Darkhouse Spearfishing

Across North America

Darkhouse Spearfishing
Across North America

By
Jay A. Leitch

Institute for Regional Studies
North Dakota State University, Fargo

To Mom and Dad

Andy C. Leitch

Andy C. Leitch

Dad only started spearing regularly after he had fully retired, although the first recollection I have of spearing is with him on Pickerel Lake (near Maine, Minnesota) when I was still pre-school age. However, once he got into it, there was no stopping him. He went to his darkhouse almost daily until the winter of 1999-2000, when, at age 76, the physical rigor of spearing became too much for him. He continues to offer me "advice" on how, when, and where to spear; and he always looks forward to fresh fried northern.

Contents

Cover: "Darkhouse Action," Les Kouba

"Darkhouse Spearing" by Les Kouba appeared on the cover of the first printing. All 3,000 original prints were sold by 1995. It has been the most popular of the darkhouse series that Kouba painted.

"Darkhouse Finale"

"Darkhouse Fish Heritage"

Available from American Wildlife Art Gallery, Minneapolis, Minnesota.

Foreword

From Subsistence to Sociability: The Evolving Traditions of Darkhouse Spearing

By Philip Nusbaum

Like all fishing, darkhouse spearing is at its core a subsistence activity. The darkhouse spearfisher entices a fish to approach a fishing hole cut in lake ice. When the opportunity arises, the fisher chucks a spear at the fish and, if the throw is on the mark, pulls the fish from the water. Once the fish is dead, the spearer both cooks and consumes it a short time after it has been caught or preserves it to eat later. However, to many participants, darkhouse spearfishing is much more than a way of procuring food. Darkhouse spearfishing exists at the intersection of politics, folklore, sociability, nostalgia, and sporting collecting. It is a mixture of an elemental activity and sophistication, an age-old activity but not overcome by the post-modern world.

Darkhouse Spearfishing Background

In cold regions, native people have fished through the ice for centuries. Because European and Native Americans today follow the same general method, many assume that European settlers in the North America learned about spear fishing from the Natives. Spearers from each group fish from a darkened space over the ice. The reason for fishing in a space darker than the water is to prohibit fish from seeing outside of the fishing hole. However, from the darkness over the fishing hole, the spearfisher can see into the hole, including any fish that swim into it. Some tribal spearers typically crouch over holes, and cover themselves and the hole with blankets, or they fish within small structures resembling small teepees. On the other hand, European North Americans typically fish within structures resembling small houses.

Changes in the Activity of Darkhouse Spearfishing

Darkhouse spearfishing is a folk cultural activity whose utilitarian accoutrements, to participants, suggest a prior age. For example, in an age where lightweight plastic seems to be the choice of industry, the spear is always made of heavy metal. Decoys are generally made by hand. If they are factory made, the factory is an improvised setup housed in someone's garage. Most darkhouses are made of a mixture of recycled materials by hands that use them, frequently with customized features such as skis mounted on an exterior wall to facilitate pulling over snow and ice.

It isn't only the implements of spearing that suggest an earlier era. Darkhouse spearfishing always involves broadening one's view regarding what constitutes an acceptable level of comfort. At the beginning of the twenty-first century, although spearfishers live in a cold climate, they are seldom cold. On the other hand, trekking even a short distance across a frozen lake to a darkhouse always involves cold air touching one's flesh, and sometimes the icy blasts can freeze one's face and ears. In addition, the spearfisher must accept that while a darkhouse furnace can warm one's body, the ice below the floorboards will always chill one's feet.

Old-timers reminisce about the solitude of the fish house, and how a darkhouse trip gave a person the opportunity to think through a vexing problem while waiting for a legal fish to swim within view of the hole. At the beginning of the twenty-first century, subsistence and solitude are darkhouse spearfishing goals that persist. However, these are not the only goals connected to darkhouse spearing. It is becoming more and more common that spearfishing expeditions are created as social occasions whose goal is to bring people together. While catching a fish is the centerpiece of a spearing expedition, all is not lost if no one spears a northern pike of substantial size. It merely means that the party will eat food it has brought, or dine in a restaurant.

The changes in darkhouse spearfishing parallel changes in other folk cultural activities. For example, although they have always been admired for their beauty, quilts used to be made primarily to provide warmth. However, today's quilters are motivated by the enjoyment of creating art objects, the symbolism of a quilt, and getting together with other quilters ahead of quilts' utilitarian function. In the early twenty-first century, some darkhouse spearfishing enthusiasts have formed voluntary associations, frequently incorporated as non-profit groups. Like other grassroots groups of bluegrass or polka music fans, quilters, or Vietnam War veterans, darkhouse spearing groups meet to socialize with others who share their interest, as well as represent their interest to the outside world.

The Significance of Darkhouse Spearfishing

Darkhouse spearfishing is important not only because it has existed over time and geography, but also because those who participate are members of an active culture. Individual spearfishers possess great knowledge of the lakes they fish, about which kinds of decoys are effective in which kinds of conditions, and about the best materials to use in building a darkhouse. By sharing this type of information with one another, darkhouse spearfishers have created and continue to create a multi-faceted experiential domain that has persisted for generations. In addition, spearers perceive themselves as keepers of a distinct cultural tradition, and they express keen interests in everything connected to darkhouse spearfishing.

Darkhouse spearfishing enthusiasts treat items such as old ice augers used to create holes in the ice, and spearfishing decoys, similarly to family heirlooms, and in many cases, they are. In addition, there is now a darkhouse spearfishing community that is confined neither by locality nor by family membership. It comprises regional groups of people with abiding interests in spearfishing, and these communities function as extended families for those who participate.

The interest in darkhouse spearfishing derives partially from its "up north" quality. Stories abound regarding the amazement of southerners introduced to darkhouse spearfishing, particularly their shock at the casual way northerners drive their vehicles across lake ice. It must also be admitted that anyone's first walk over lake ice is unforgettable. Knowing and experiencing the footing, hearing the sounds made by the subtle movements of the ice, and feeling the cold air sear one's face make travel by foot over lake ice seem like taking a walk on another planet. Spearfishers express fascination with the peculiar glow that emanates out of a fishing hole, and excitement at pulling a big northern pike out of the water.

For some, the attraction to darkhouse spearing manifests itself in collections of items associated with the pastime. The most highly collected type of item is the spearfishing decoy. There exists a network of outdoor collectables shows, each containing booths where collectors buy and sell decoys along with such items as old shot shell cases, antique fishing reels, and old magazines connected to the outdoors. Many of the collectors of spearing decoys are themselves darkhouse spearers whose collecting is motivated by a combination of sentiment for darkhouse spearfishing, an aesthetic appreciation of spearfishing decoys, and an understanding of their value on the collectors' market. Collectors regard spearfishing decoys generally as folk art products of a cultural tradition, and especially prize the artistry of certain master decoy makers such as Oscar Peterson. Because most of the old decoys have been collected up, there is interest in contemporary-made decoys. Certain artists such as Dave Kober of Bear Lake, Michigan, and John Jensen of Frazee, Minnesota, are back ordered with requests from collectors.

The Future of Darkhouse Spearfishing

In the early twenty-first century, there are multiple means of enjoying darkhouse spearfishing. One can enjoy the pastime solo, participate in groups, and enter into the concerted action of voluntary associations. However, despite the vibrancy of the scene, the future of darkhouse spearfishing rests to a great degree on the legal system. Spearing has its critics, but recent legislative history registers an expansion of its domain: in April 2000 the state of North Dakota legalized darkhouse spearfishing.

Why this Book is Important

While northern citizens see themselves conversant in such modern matters as silicon chips, they also consider themselves rugged outdoors folk who relish encountering nature on nature's terms. Winter is their defining season, and despite or because of the season's length and severity, people view winter as something to do something with. One look at the large number of darkhouses erected on certain lakes tells how many elect to spend winter. Perhaps nothing captures the northern spirit like winter fishing.

Darkhouse spearfishing is a tradition extending through many northern states. However, it receives little attention from official gatekeepers such as the chambers of commerce, the academy, and mass media that form a cultural infrastructure. Part of the reason is that it is a folk tradition, and very few mainstream entities speak for folk phenomena. Occasionally the mass media delivers a program that stokes interest in a folk tradition, as when the movie *A River Runs Through It*, briefly gave fly-fishing a day in the sun in the 1990s.

This book is important because it provides the most comprehensive information available regarding a folk cultural tradition that has stood the test of time. The coming chapters tell, in plain language, about the essentials of darkhouse spearfishing. They deliver history, folklore, theory, regional variations, and a close telling of how practitioners make it happen. Jay Leitch has delivered the definitive treatment of spearing, told in a way that is factual, yet also relates to the depth of feeling the old-timers have for the sport. Darkhouse spearers and their friends have eagerly awaited this revised edition of *Darkhouse Spearfishing Across North America*. Leitch's superior reporting displays that it was well worth the wait.

Philip Nusbaum is Folklorist, Minnesota State Arts Board, and a scholar of the material culture of winter fishing.

Acknowledgements

Many people have helped me put this volume together. My wife, Becky, has been patient and accepting of the fact that I needed, on occasion, to collect data in the field, or should I say on the ice. She became almost as enthusiastic about spearing as I am. She endured my hours of writing and library research. But most of all, she encouraged me to complete what I think is my most important publication.

My son, Philip, helped with data collection, although he isn't much interested in fishing. My parents, Andy and Carol, encouraged my early interest in spearing, allowing me to build several darkhouses and to flirt with early winter ice. My father is always eager to eat northerns and no one can fry them better than my mother. Each of them also contributed in many ways to the completion of this book, visiting with people in the community and searching in libraries and newspaper archives.

I appreciate the help of many librarians, especially those in the Library of Congress and at North Dakota State University, who helped with my searches.

Several reviewers provided many useful suggestions. My long time buddy, Les Cordes, contributed his insights as a fellow darkhouse fisherman. Arlen Harmoning read a draft with his usual critical eye. Darla Christensen read a draft with the eyes of a complete novice, thereby providing me with some useful suggestions.

Each of the state sections was reviewed by at least one game and fish professional from that state, including: Michael J. Kramer, Alaska Department of Fish and Game; Art Talsma and Robert Hanten, South Dakota Department of Game, Fish and Parks; Robert Needham, Montana Department of Fish, Wildlife, and Parks; Ned Fogle, Michigan Department of Natural Resources; John Klingbid, Wisconsin Department of Natural Resources; and Paul "Jack" Wingate, Minnesota Department of Natural Resources.

I owe thanks to my staff at work, who found time to help out with data collection, analysis, and many trips to the library. They include Theresa Golz, Lila Borge, Jim Baltezore, and Carmen Norskog.

Finally, Debbie Tanner turned my rough sketches into drawings. She turned my draft into a book. She deserves a very special thanks for making it all come together.

A note to my students and to other would-be writers: It took a long, long time to bring this book to press. Getting ideas from the brain to paper is no easy task. Sure, there were many other distractions, like work and fishing, but writing takes time. Each page of this book has gone through countless iterations. The chapters were reordered several times until they finally seemed to fit together. And there might still be errors in form and logic!

Of course, I accept full responsibility for any errors that remain in style, grammar, logic, or substance. I also apologize in advance to anyone I might offend by not always being gender neutral in my writing. I am sensitive to the issues, and I tried!

Acknowledgments to the Second Printing

Thanks to all those who bought and read the First Edition and to the many who sent me letters about their own experiences in the darkhouse.

Of course, I again acknowledge all those who helped with the First Printing — Thanks! The most thanks for help with this edition go to the leadership of the Minnesota Darkhouse & Anglers Association, who persisted in asking about a second printing until they wore me down.

Others who were instrumental and deserve recognition and thanks include Barb Geeslin, who retyped the text of the first edition; Debbie Tanner, who pulled the text, figures, and photos into an electronic file ready for the printer; and my wife, Becky, who helped with the additional data collection and served as an objective editorial critic.

Roger Goeschel and Eric Swenson of the Metro Chapter of MD&AA and all the members of the Lakes (Detroit Lakes) Chapter of MD&AA who first encouraged me and then partnered with me to produce this edition–thanks to each of you.

J.A.L.

Preface to the Second Printing

It has been nearly ten years since I wrote the first edition of *Darkhouse Spearfishing Across North America*. The 1,000 copies of the first edition, printed in 1992, were sold out by late 1996. They were sold to spearing enthusiasts, book stores, libraries, bait shops, friends, and others as far away as Alaska, New England, and California. Thank you! However, there is still a strong demand for this little book, so with the encouragement of the Minnesota Darkhouse & Angling Association I decided to reprint it. That wasn't as easy as I thought. First, the original print shop had not retained the "print ready" pages. Second, the quality of the photographs would not be adequate if we just printed from the book. Third, I work for a living and it is slow getting around to hobby projects that take time and effort. Obviously, we did reprint, but in the process the book had to be retyped and, basically, done over.

Many parts of the first printing appeared in *Jackfish Journal* and other local outdoor sports newspapers. *Fur-Fish-Game* magazine published a summary in 1994 ("Darkhouse Spearfishing," *Fur-Fish-Game* 91(2):12-15) and some photos were published in *Outdoor Life* magazine (January 1997).

The Second Printing contains all the text that was in the First Edition, but without the typos. I have added text in several areas, especially the chapters on Alaska and South Dakota, and have included some additional photos. Unfortunately, some of the photos in the original edition could not be included because I couldn't find them, or I had returned them.

Much has happened since the first printing. Ice fishing technology has "advanced," including the availability of Global Positioning Systems (GPS), through the ice depth finders, underwater video cameras, cell phones, and far more gear is available from commercial vendors. North Dakota has legalized "spearfishing through the ice from dark houses." The World Wide Web (www) is a fantastic resource for finding information regarding fishing opportunities, researching and buying equipment, selling decoys on e-bay, chatting about fishing, and even buying licenses.

Part I
Background

CHAPTER 1
Introduction

Native Americans were spearing fish through the ice long before Europeans reached North America. But it is difficult to pin down the precise origin of darkhouse spearing. Several ideas are offered in the history discussed in Chapter 2.

Darkhouse spearing is very serene in practice. But, mention darkhouse spearing and many people get excited, some because they have experienced spearing first hand, others because they think spearing should be outlawed. Spearing is a hotly debated subject in Minnesota, where nearly 25,000 residents buy spearing licenses each year. Their numbers pale when compared to approximately 700,000 other winter anglers and the 2 million who fish during the summer. The dimensions of this ongoing controversy are reviewed in Chapter 3.

Darkhouse spearing is as much a tradition as it is a sport for many who participate. Locals who were busy with farmwork or the tourist business in summer can relax in a warm darkhouse while waiting for a big one to swim into view. Darkhouses, spears, decoys, techniques, and favorite fishing spots are passed along to younger generations. The darkhouse spearer's equipment is discussed in Chapters 4 and 5.

Darkhouses on a Minnesota lake.

Imagine the underwater tranquility of a freshwater lake covered with two feet of ice under a soft blanket of snow. Many sportsmen are observers of that tranquil scene, sitting in darkened fish shanties peering through large holes cut, drilled, or chopped through the ice. Just as the peaceful serenity of a dozen playful perch or sunfish is about to lull you into a very relaxed state of consciousness, the stillness is shattered by the explosive appearance of the most vicious freshwater predator — the northern pike. The only noise, however, is the pounding heart of the fisherman groping for the spear before the prey disappears as fast as it appeared. It is, then, with spear in hand, waiting and wondering if the fish will return, that the excitement of this winter sport reaches its peak.

This scene is played out by fewer and fewer fishermen on fewer and fewer lakes each year as darkhouse fishing is losing out to the pressures of anglers and resort owners. Although there are now only 40 lakes closed to spearing in Minnesota, they represent a disproportionate amount of the state's spearing opportunity. This book was compiled to provide a description, a history, and an objective look at this unique form of winter recreation. The idea to write this book came to me during the winter of 1985-86, while on a year-long assignment in Washington, D.C. Writing about spearing was one way to satisfy my urge to go spearing that winter.

I wrote this book because none existed that covered darkhouse spearing from A to Z. I also wrote it because the public cannot expect to learn much from spearers themselves. It is well known that fishermen tell fish stories — they lie! For example, the caption under the newspaper photo of a friend

SPEARED –
Gary Harrington, Battle Lake, speared this 23½ pound northern on Pickerel Lake Friday afternoon. Harrington is home on leave from the Army and hadn't speared in the past four years. His 43-inch northern was speared on the first day he went spearing. *Note: He actually speared it on Twin Lake and he was home on leave from the Navy!*

holding a 24-pound northern said it was speared in a lake 5 miles from where his darkhouse was! Although I used fishermen as a source of information, I wasn't foolish enough to rely solely on them.

There is also something different about spearers; they are less social than anglers and more secretive about their success or lack thereof. Darkhouse spearing is usually a one-person activity. There is no card playing, no social activity, and no story telling. Spearing is the spearer, his own thoughts, and the activity going on in the lake below. Chapter 6 describes darkhouse spearing and just what makes people brave the cold and hazards of ice-covered lakes to participate.

Spearing was practiced — or at least, was not illegal — in many states including some in New England until the early 20th Century. However spearing is legal in only seven states today. Minnesota, Montana, South Dakota, Michigan, Alaska, and Wisconsin have allowed winter darkhouse spearing for game fish for quite a while. North Dakota legalized winter spearing in 2001. Minnesota spearers like to get out early, before the ice gets very thick and while the whitefish are spawning. On the other hand, Michigan, Montana, and Alaska spearers think that late winter is best, when the big females are moving into the shallows in anticipation of spring. Seasons, species, and methods vary somewhat, but the thrill is the same no matter what state you're in or what lake you're peering into.

Nowhere outside of Minnesota are there as many spearers, nor is spearing so controversial. In fact, there are more darkhouse spearers in Minnesota than in the other six states combined. On the other hand, Minnesota also has the most restrictive spearing regulations, while Wisconsin has the fewest areas open to spearing.

Although darkhouse spearing is relatively safe when compared to many other sports, there are some risks, and some lives are lost every year by careless or unlucky ice fishermen. Chapter 14 covers some important safety considerations.

The purpose of this book is to record darkhouse spearing as a part of American heritage before it becomes a lost tradition. I have tried to put it in an objective setting so that decisions about its future can be based, not on emotion, but on a more complete knowledge and appreciation of the activity. The final chapter, Chapter 15, draws some conclusions about darkhouse spearing and speculates about its future.

I have concentrated on darkhouse spearing for northern pike, but deviate now and then to discuss sturgeon, muskie, or other species, and open-water spearing. Common names of fish, or at least the most common names used in the Midwest, are used throughout the book. Overhead profiles of fish species seen most often in the darkhouse, as seen from above by the darkhouse spearer, are shown on page 8, along with their more common, side profiles.

This book is not meant to be a scholarly research report, although I have been careful to annotate my sources and have tried to be objective (sort of!). Information used to develop the book came from three primary sources. First, I consulted the usual printed sources in numerous libraries, using materials in the stacks and from computerized literature searches. Next, as you will see, I drew heavily on my own experiences as a darkhouse spearer over the past four decades. Finally, conversations with spearers, friends and families of spearers, bait and sporting goods store operators, and professional fish management personnel round out my information sources.

Page through the book and look at the pictures and drawings to get a feeling for darkhouse spearing before you read the text. Reading this book will not be nearly as exciting as the actual experience of being in a darkhouse, but neither will reading be as much work as cutting big holes through the ice. But it will help to develop a fuller appreciation for the sport, the issues, and the people involved.

Common name (scientific name), and other regional names of fish referred to in this book

BASS (*Micropterus dolomieui* [smallmouth], *M. salmoides* [largemouth])

BULLHEAD (*Icalurus melas* [black], *I. nebulosus* [brown], *I. Natalis* [yellow])

CARP (*Cyprinus carpio*), German carp, European carp, Asian carp

CATFISH (*Ictalurus punctatus* [channel], *I. furcatus* [blue])

CRAPPIE (*Pomoxis nigromaculatus* [black], *P. annularis* [white])

CREEK CHUB (*Semotilus atromaculatus*)

DOGFISH (*Amia calva*), bowfin

EELPOUT (*Lota lota*), burbot, freshwater cod, lawyer, loche, ling, cusk, dogfish, gudgeon, maria

GAR (*Lepisosteus osseus* [long nose], *L. platostomus* [short nose])

GRAYLING (*Thymallus arcticus*)

LAKE STURGEON (*Acipenser fulvescens*), freshwater sturgeon, rock sturgeon, stone sturgeon, red sturgeon, ruddy sturgeon, shell-back sturgeon, smoothback

MUSKELLUNGE (*Esox masquinongy*), muskie, musky

NORTHERN PIKE (*Esox lucius*), pike, great northern pike, jack, jackfish, jackpike, pickerel, northern, river lizard, common pike, snake, hammer handle, slimy SOB, snot rocket, slough sharks, water wolf, gators, picklers

REDHORSE (*Maxostoma* [six species])

SAUGER (*Stizostedion canadense*)

SHINER (*Notropis cornutus* [common], *Notemigonus crysoleucas* [golden])

SUCKER (*Catostomus commersonii*)

SUNFISH (*Lepomis* [five species]), bluegill, pumpkinseed, panfish

YELLOW PERCH (*Perca flavescens*)

WALLEYE (*Stizostedion vitreum*), pike, 'eyes

WHITEFISH (*Coregonus clupeaformis*), tullibee, cisco

Profiles of things seen in the darkhouse.

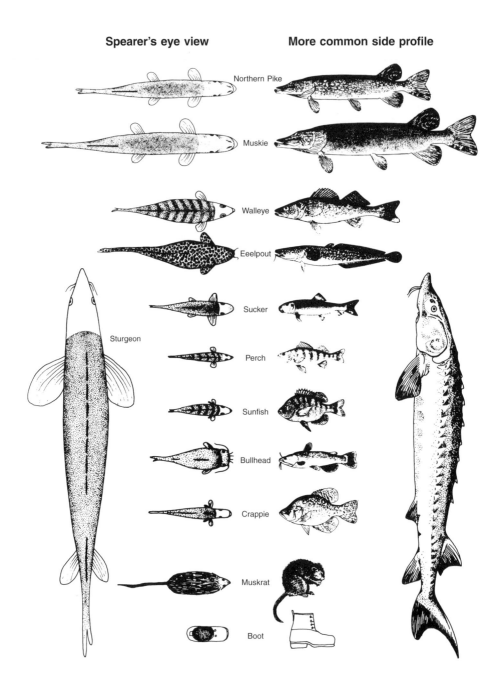

Spearer's eye view   More common side profile

Northern Pike

Muskie

Walleye

Eeelpout

Sucker

Perch

Sturgeon

Sunfish

Bullhead

Crappie

Muskrat

Boot

CHAPTER 2
History

Humans have fished for as long as their activities can be traced (Radcliffe 1921). Fishing was first done out of a need to survive, only much later it became a sport — something to be done to relax and to enjoy the out-of-doors. Nevertheless, some fishing is still done on a subsistence or commercial basis to supply much needed foodstuffs.

Humans have fished for centuries and continue to fish, using a wide variety of techniques (Radcliffe 1921, von Brandt 1964). Perhaps the most primitive is simply grasping by hand or through the use of trained animals, such as cormorants or even dogs. Some of the first fishing "tools" included spears, harpoons, blow-pipes, clubs, and traps. Stupefying methods, such as poisons and explosives have been used. Any number of nets, trawls, and dredges have been developed. The most common technique, and that most popular with today's sport angler is, of course, the hook and line.

Spearfishing might be one of the oldest forms of fishing done by man (Chiappetta 1966), predating angling, especially angling as a sport (Trench 1974). "Ancient artifacts show natives

27-pound "pickeral" speared by Julius Anderson at Norway Lake (Otter Tail County, Minnesota).

in various poses in the act of casting spears at fish beneath the water,... (Little 1975)." Spearfishing was especially common in tropical seas and along sea-coasts where fish congregated to spawn. This earliest method of spearfishing was done out of necessity — to provide food.

A special kind of recreational winter spearfishing exists in North America today; where the spearer sits in a darkhouse on a frozen lake or river waiting for the prey to be attracted into range by a decoy hanging several feet below the surface of the ice in the clear water below.

The origin of through-the-ice spearing is uncertain. Spearfishing, in general, was thought to have been independently introduced in many places around the world; no single location can be credited with its introduction. The introduction of through-the-ice spearing would have a narrower geographic range, and may have been introduced at a point and dispersed or was independently introduced at many points. It could have began in northern Asia, North America, or northern Europe.

Asian Origin?

Old Japanese silk paintings show Ainu spearing through the ice under semiconical mat dark tents (Rostlund 1952). Tribes in Siberia also used fish decoys, perhaps linking through-the-ice spearing to North America via the Bering Straits. Although, the spear was used infrequently as a fishing device in China (Radcliffe 1921).

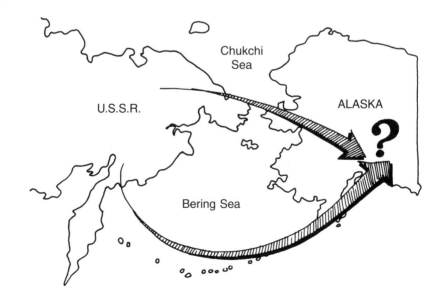

Scandinavian Origin?

It is tempting to speculate that darkhouse spearing came to North America with the Scandinavian ancestors of modern day spearers. Norway, Finland, and Sweden have hundreds of clear lakes and fjords with large populations of huge northern pike. Northerns are more popular as game fish in Scandinavia than in the United States, and ice fishing is common throughout northern Europe (Ormstad and Rom 1972). However, no evidence exists to suggest darkhouse spearing was practiced in Scandinavia, nor does it exist there today, although the Danes spear eels through the ice (von Brandt 1964).

North American Origin?

The next thought might be that we learned it from the North American Indians who inhabited the colder northern regions. Every school child knows that Indians speared fish during spring, summer, and fall (Densmore 1979). (They still do in some places, see Chapter 13.) There is extensive evidence that Native Americans speared fish through the ice from darkened "houses" after attracting them with an artificial decoy. Native American houses were made of blankets, brush, or snow.

Eskimos also speared fish through the ice after they attracted the fish into view with various types of decoys (Mary-Rousseliere 1971). The Kimballs (1986) reported that Eskimos, Athabascans, British Columbia's interior Indians, Northwest Coast Indians, and Great Lakes Indians all used decoys, but that it was the Great Lakes Indians who introduced winter spearing to European settlers.

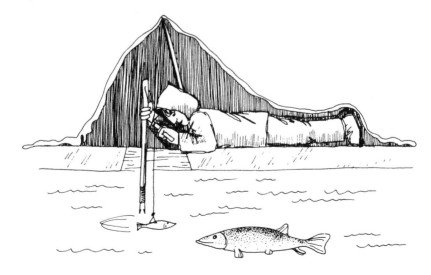

The Kimballs (1986) speculate that darkhouse spearing originated in North America, and was then dispersed to Asia, since fish decoys have not been found very far into Asia. Rostlund (1952) concludes that darkhouse spearing is old, since it is so widely dispersed, but he offers no insights into its origin.

Stark and Berglund (1990, p. 113) note "Though spear fishing dates back to prehistoric times, the fish decoy appeared on the scene in the 1890s in Alaska Eskimo communities, and soon after it appeared in the lower states." The dispersal idea is perhaps correct, but the decoy appeared much earlier than the 1890s.

In his *History of the Ojibway People* (first published in 1885), Warren (1984) writes:

One clear morning in the early part of winter, soon after the islands, which are clustered in this portion of Lake Superior and known as the Apostles, had been locked in ice, a party of young men of the Ojibways started out from their village in the Bay of Shag-a-waum-ik-ong, to go, as was customary, and spear fish through holes in the ice, between the island of La Pointe and the main shore, this being considered as the best ground for this mode of fishing. (p. 121)

Frances Densmore, a prominent figure in the study of American Indian culture, wrote in her book (1979) on Chippewa (Ojibway) customs:

Fish were secured by the following means: (1) By the use of seines; (2) by spearing at night with a torch; (3) by spearing through the ice with a decoy; (4) by traps; (5) by the use of bait; (6) by fishhooks; and (7) by trolling. (p. 125)

Densmore continues:

(3) Spearing through the ice with a decoy: The decoy fish were made of wood with a tail of birch bark and body weighted with lead. Some skill was required in making these so that their equilibrium in the water was perfect. When using them the Indian cut a hole in the ice and lay flat beside it with his face over the opening. His head and shoulders were covered by a blanket, which frequently was supported by a tripod or frame of sticks. With his left hand he guided the decoy so that its movements would be as lifelike as possible, and in his right hand he held the spear ready to strike at the proper moment. (p. 126)

Ice chisels and double-barbed iron spears were among items traded to Indians in the northern latitudes for their beaver pelts in a 1779 account (Wheeler 1985). Indians could trade one bear pelt for two of North West Company's ice chizzels [sic]. Spears were mounted on wooden poles and used for spearing muskrats, beaver, and large fish. Nineteen wrought-iron ice chisels and six double-barbed iron spears were recovered from the Basswood River in northern Minnesota in July 1961, perhaps lost when an 18th Century trader's canoe overturned.

The Sioux were also wintertime spearers, as Lindquist and Clark's (1937, p.16) citation of Reverend Samuel W. Pond's book, *The Sioux As They Were in Minnesota in 1834*, records:

In the winter they cut holes through the ice, and, crouching down with their blankets spread over them to exclude the light, waited patiently for the fish to approach the aperture where they could spear them. Sometimes they used bows and arrows instead of spears, a string being attached to the arrow so that it might be drawn back again. Winter fishing was most practiced by the upper Indians, they sometimes depending a long time on fish alone for subsistence. It was tedious, dreary work on the large lakes in cold weather....

The Kimballs (1986) claim that "When settlers and explorers came to the U.S.A. [sic] they found the fish decoy already in use by native people (p. vii)." Michigan, Minnesota, New York, and Wisconsin had sufficient ice, food fish, tradition, knowledge of techniques, and game laws to allow winter spearing. The Kimballs discuss Alexander Henry's introduction to spearing in the late 1700s, Gurdon Hubbard's in Michigan's Muskegon Lake in 1819, Henry Schoolcraft's in Saginaw Bay in 1820 and other times among several different Indian tribes, and Alanson Skinner's accounts of Menominee Indians spearing in Wisconsin.

The Kimball's two volumes (1986, 1987) on fish decoys are an excellent introduction to the use and to the variety of decoys produced over time. Chapter two of volume one (Kimballs 1986, pp. 49-60) is "The Early History" of decoys and spearing.

Boulanger (1971) reported that farther north in Manitoba, winter fishing was also practiced. "That time [winter] in Lake Winnipeg, they were always winter fishing, Icelanders and Indians, all over in lake Winnipeg" (pp. 33-34). "And to keep the fresh fish so we can sell it in the winter time, we would make a good snowhouse in the lake. Same thing as Eskimos do...." (pp. 65-66)

Becker County, in West Central Minnesota, is easily one of the most popular darkhouse spearing counties in Minnesota, if not, the country. Winter spearing was practiced there as early as the turn of the 20th Century, as reported by Wilcox in 1907: "The pickerel is easily caught, for it will bite at anything; and during the winter is speared through holes in the ice" (p. 193).

The *Henning Advocate* (Henning, Minnesota) of February 21, 1913 reported:

> *Nick Thill is exhibiting a 12-pound pickerel that he speared in Battle Lake. House fishermen report that fish are moving better than they did the fore part of the winter.*

The *American and Canadian Sportsman's Encyclopedia of Valuable Instruction*, published by the American and Canadian Sportsman's Association in 1913, described pickerel (N. Pike) spearing: "In winter a dark tent or house box is placed on the ice ponds and the interior darkened; a hole is then cut in the ice so as to observe the fish, which is lured to within spear point by means of a decoy minnow" (p. 217). A drawing of 'pickerel spearing in winter' was also included.

The 1908 *Sears, Roebuck & Company Catalogue* shows four different fish spears for sale (Schroeder 1969). *William Mills and Son 1905 Catalog* also offered commercially made fish spears (William Mills 1905). Spears will be covered in more detail in Chapter 5.

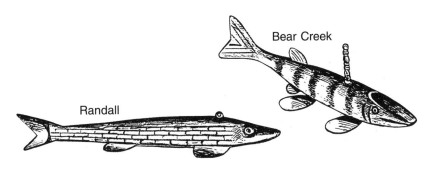

Two early commercially made fish decoys.

Commercially made decoys were available too at the turn of the Century (Kimballs 1986, 1987). Collectors have only in the past 25 or 30 years recognized decoys as important indicators of a part of our American heritage as well as the culture of Native Americans. (Chapter 5 has more to say about spearing decoys.)

I received a letter from Duane Esarey, an archaeologist interested in the origins of decoy fishing, in July 1993, shortly after publication of the First Edition. At the time Mr. Esarey was the collections manager for Dickson Mounds Museum in Lewiston, Illinois. He wrote:

> Dear Jay,
>
> I recently saw a book on decoy fishing that you have published. ...(I)t was by far the most scholarly and definitive work out on the subject. I doubt if it will be surpassed in the near future. *[Author's note: I couldn't resist including that!]*
>
> Basically, I find that the practice has been ethnographically observed all through North America from Eastern Greenland to the Bering Straits and all through the eastern half of Asia (at least as far west as 80 degrees longitude). In each hemisphere the practice is ethnographically documented as far south as about 40 degrees latitude.
>
> Archaeologically, the distribution is approximately the same, except I have not looked into the Asian archaeology sufficiently to document it south of lake Baikal at ca. 50 degrees latitude.... Archaeological

decoys are made of shell, stone, bone, and ivory (plus wood in several instances and copper in one case). I have been able to find no evidence that the practice is older than about 1000 years in North America, while it goes back as far as 4500 years in central Asia.

Mr. Esarey also summarized his findings about the history of decoy fishing in an article in *The Living Museum* in 1993 (Esarey 1993).

Conclusion

Clearly, darkhouse spearing as we know it today evolved from what was passed on to European settlers by Native North Americans (Zumbro 1978). Whether an early form of through-the-ice spearing dispersed southeast from the Eskimos or dispersed northwest from the Great Lakes tribes is a matter for anthropologists. How through-the-ice spearing got to North America — whether it evolved independently or was dispersed from Asia via the Aleutian land bridge — also remains unresolved. What is known, however, is that given the ideal natural conditions for ice fishing in the area of the Great Lakes, it probably wasn't long after the last glacial period, about 10,000 years ago, that the first fish was speared through the ice.

■

*God does not deduct from man's life
the days spent fishing.*

CHAPTER 3
The Controversy

■

*Let us engage in the serious business
of conducting our discussion
rationally and logically to discover the truth
about points on which we differ.* (Adler 1990)

Darkhouse spearing has been and remains extremely controversial in Minnesota, although never violent to my knowledge, since the early sixties. It hasn't been very controversial in any of the other five states, yet there have been controversies about Native American spearing activities in Wisconsin (see Chapter 13) and more recently, in Minnesota. This chapter presents a hopefully sober, scientific, and unbiased analysis of the darkhouse spearing controversy.

About 40 of Minnesota's 10,000 lakes are closed to darkhouse spearing because they are managed for muskellunge.

There are two general groups opposed to darkhouse spearing — summer sport anglers who claim it isn't sport and resort owners who want to save the fish for tourists. Many special interest groups, such as Muskies, Inc., openly oppose spearing as well as some influential individuals, like the former editor of *Outdoor News,* Jim Peterson. "Harpooning is the biggest obstacle to improving fishing and improving the tourist industry" (Peterson 1985). Peterson has been a persistent opponent of spearing, inciting others with his anti-spearing editorials. Under new editorship, *Outdoor News* is no longer hostile toward spearing.

It is surprising that many spearing detractors don't even like to fish for, much less catch, northerns. Most anglers detest "slimy green" northerns and would rather catch walleyes or crappies. Only 3 percent of nearly 1800 anglers interviewed while winter fishing in Minnesota (in three Wright County lakes) in 1985-86 were fishing for northerns; nearly 45 percent were after crappies (Treat 1987). Minnesota anglers prefer walleyes to northerns by a five to one margin (Baltezore and Leitch 1987).

Controversies often result from misunderstanding, poor information, or proposed changes in the *status quo.* All three contribute to the darkhouse spearing issue. The controversy revolves mainly around four issues: Whether or not spearing is a sporting way to fish for pleasure. Whether or not spearers take a disproportionate number of large fish. Whether spearers cripple too many fish. And, whether or not spearers take illegal fish, such as muskies and walleyes.

Minnesota's DNR has never taken an official stand against darkhouse spearing; however, some DNR employees doubt if its future is very bright. Joe Alexander, former DNR Commissioner, once said "If politicians and future politicians of this area [Bemidji, Minnesota] continue to support spearing, they would be better off to put their money on Gary Hart in the presidential race" (*The Fourm* 1987).

Beliefs

Strongly held beliefs about the pros or cons of darkhouse spearing are often in the minds of "vulgar believers," one of three types of believers. Vulgar believers aren't interested in facts or logic; they support their causes and know they are correct (Ruggiero 1998). Sophisticated believers are a bit more rational, but are also strongly behind their causes and won't change their minds. Sophisticated believers are able to bring facts, figures, and logic to support their points of view. Finally, critical believers are well informed about the issues and base their beliefs on facts, figures, and well thought out arguments. They are willing to alter their beliefs if additional information is provided that changes the conclusions. This book was written for all three types of believers.

Is it Sport?

Opponents of darkhouse spearing don't believe "harpooning" is a fair way to take game fish. Fish do not even have to bite, they only need to be lured into view before being harpooned from above. There is no fair chase. The fish don't have a chance to fight back and may only be wounded or maimed. There is no skill involved (Bergh 1975).

There are even religious arguments against spearing fish:

It is told on the Turkish Black Sea coast that in the Koran is a story about a blasphemer who wanted to kill the Lord. When he was shooting an arrow, angels were ordered to keep a fish in the way of the missile and the fish was pierced instead of God. In gratitude for this service the Lord ordered that never more should a fish be pierced by spear or arrow (von Brandt 1964, p. 25).

Sporting? The spearing controversy is similar in ways to anti-hunting arguments, and neither science nor logic can reach a definitive, logical conclusion. It boils down to a question of values, which are part of human culture. And, in a democracy, to who can marshall the greatest number of votes for their particular point of view; especially when resources (fish, for example) are not plentiful enough for everyone who wants a share.

Aldo Leopold said that sport is whatever the participant believes it is. He argued that as long as the activity was within certain bounds, anglers or hunters could use whatever means they desired to capture their legal limits.

Aldo Leopold, and George Bird Grinnell forty years before him, warned that sportsmen should not create, or tolerate, the creation of laws with any other motive than protecting the renewability of gamebirds, fish, and mammals. The kinds of equipment or methods used to take game are matters of local custom and conscience, not legislation. (Reiger 1988)

In a related argument, Causey (1989, p. 331) talks about the morality of hunting, saying, "There is no one activity that we can define as hunting *per se*,..." The same could be said about fishing. Causey (p. 343) also notes "...the greatest satisfaction of having the opportunity to kill game is to let it go." No fisherman knows this better than the darkhouse spearer, who has the opportunity to "let fish go" without the fish even knowing it. Catch-and-release at its best! However, some claim it is more difficult for the darkhouse spearer to "let one go by" than it might be for an angler to release one, or even for a sport hunter to let a legal buck go by. I can't agree.

In 1873, Jacobstaff (1873 p. 252) found spearing to be more exciting than winter angling. "...neither of these methods [angling] compare with that of spearing fish in winter,...[spearing] requires so much skill and dexterity that it may be included with legitimate sports."

Rau (1977) wrote in *Sports Illustrated.*

Spearing may seem like a primitive, almost barbaric way of taking a legitimate game fish in this the age of electronic fish finders and graphite rods and $6000 bass boats. But that just might be the attraction. Taking a fish in the oldest way known to man. Before hook and line, before rod and reel. Before ultra-light spincasting gear and electronic lures. A spear. There is something clean and simple and pure at work. There is a sense of being removed from technology sitting inside a darkened box on a frozen lake viewing the timelessness of the lake bottom...(p. 38)

Zumbro (1978) addresses the question of whether or not spearers take unfair advantage of fish. While some anglers, especially muskie enthusiasts, maintain only hook-and-line should be used, spearers feel it takes great skill, patience, and know-how to be a good spearer. Speared fish may even suffer less than those caught by hook-and-line. Zumbro (1978, p. 159) concludes that there are no sports that have the blessings of everyone and treats "...spearing as a viable, skillful practice that is a wholesome icefishing activity."

> *...those who degrade spearing fail to see the sport in it. And there is sport in spearing! You cannot believe the thrill of SEEING a big northern coming into view. The thrill of seeing that fish is tremendous. (Fellegy 1975)*

While, two wrongs don't make it right, how sporting is hunting ducks over decoys? or calling turkeys? or fishing with more than one line? or bass boats, downriggers, graphs, graphite rods, underwater video cameras, and computer reels? Vermont even has a fish shooting season! Some deer hunters use long bows, others use semiautomatic .300 magnums with 9-power scopes. Which is more sporting? Darkhouse spearing is an historical and traditional method of fishing. Darkhouse spearers still use essentially the same equipment that they did 50 years ago. Is it a legitimate, sporting method of recreational fishing? You be the judge (try to be a critical believer).

Wounding fish may happen because of poor equipment, poor aim, or just plain spearing at fish out of range. I have lost some fish, only a few, because they weren't well hit. It happens. Wounded fish either die or heal with scars to the disgust of the angler.

The chance of wounding or crippling cannot be denied. However, neither can it be expected that spear wounds contribute to the reductions in fish populations any more than hook-and-line induced mortality through excessive "playing" of fish, improper handling, or releasing fish when hooks have damaged them beyond recovery. "Catch-and-release" doesn't always work with angling either. In fact, the Wisconsin DNR assumes a 15 percent hooking mortality (Meyer 1991).

Do Spearers Take the Big Fish?

There is some evidence to support the contention that darkhouse spearers harvest larger fish, on average, than do anglers (*Outdoor Outlines* 1987, Sonnenburg undated). However, for each study that reports that spearers take larger fish, there is another study that doesn't produce any such evidence. One study found that spearers took northerns that were, on average, 4 pounds heavier than those caught by anglers. Another study found spearers took northerns averaging 2.0 pounds, while anglers took northerns averaging 1.9 pounds, a difference hardly worth worrying about. A recent study on a few Minnesota lakes concluded "...that spearers were not taking a disproportionate number of large pike. Spearing is not having an impact..." (Klick 1991, p. 26).

The difference in fish sizes taken by anglers versus spearers depends heavily on the characteristics of the lake and its fish populations and on characteristics of the two groups of fishermen. In some areas the spearers have more experience and are more knowledgeable about the lakes — they are the "locals." While, the anglers might be tourists, who oftentimes catch fish only by accident.

DNR surveys have shown that spearers are more selective than anglers, letting the small ones go by. Anglers, on the other hand, have little control over what takes their lures and baits. Anglers can release small fish, but must keep some that are too badly injured to release. Also, anglers do not typically fish for big fish. Sure, they want to catch big fish, but they usually fish with baits and lures that would be more work than they are worth for a big fish.

Even though spearers may take larger fish, they do not take that many and they have been spearing in some lakes for well over 50 years, with no apparent effect. I tell anglers they've had all spring, summer, and fall to catch them. What they didn't catch, I now have a chance to spear. Spearers do not take fish away from anglers; they merely harvest a few of those that the anglers could not catch. Some MN DNR fisheries managers see spearing as another means of harvesting a fish crop that would otherwise not be used. My point exactly.

It is not unreasonable to suggest that spearers take bigger fish, leaving fewer big fish for anglers. The big fish are most likely females who contribute the most to propagating the species. It is likely that the big fish are females, but they may not make the contributions that some people think they do. On the other hand, some fishery managers claim that the bulk (up to 90 percent) of the egg-laying by northern pike is done by young, two-or three-pound females. The older and larger females contribute only a minor portion of the eggs (*Fins & Feathers* 1975).

A Minnesota DNR flyer on spearing concludes (Sonnenburg undated):

Opponents of spearing claim that spearers take mostly big female pike. This affects future pike populations they argue. It is true that most large pike are females and that eggs are very evident in the fish as the spawning season approaches. However, taking pike in the winter by spearing has no more impact on future fish populations than does catching fish by hook-and-line during any time of the year. Why? Because pike carry immature eggs in their bodies all year. Taking them in the summer has as much influence on spawning as does taking them in the winter. The fact that spearers and anglers remove fish from a lake seems to have no relationship on angling success the next summer in the same lake.

Anglers also harvest big northerns. Gerrit and Jim Kiel are among Minnesota's most successful northern pike anglers (Fellegy 1975). They report catching limits of northerns, none under 14 pounds, some over 20 pounds. The Kiel's also harvest many big northerns by spearing, but they say they prefer to angle.

Some anglers claim that the number of large northerns taken in summer has increased in designated muskie lakes where spearing is not permitted. The converse is also true: there are fewer taken in winter. So who has the greater "right?" And why didn't summer anglers catch them before freeze up, prior to the spearing ban? In fact, the angling season for northerns in Minnesota is about 10 months long and the spearing season is only about 75 days long.

In 1988, a 10-year ban on spearing was imposed on Cass Lake, Minnesota (in Beltrami and Cass Counties), after an economic study (Armson 1986) showed less money was generated by spearers than by summer anglers, and three of 77 netted muskies had spear wounds. The study's findings have been stretched well beyond the scope of the research. Outlawing spearing would not likely increase summer revenues, it would only reduce the total by the amount not spent by winter spearers. Unfortunately, this study made its impact and was quickly quoted by the sophisticated believers.

The Minnesota DNR reviewed its Cass Lake spearing ban in 1997 and extended it in spite of not having any convincing evidence to support it. The Bemidji Area Fisheries Office of DNR did a study that it said showed there was an positive impact on the size of muskies caught in Cass Lake during the ban ("Cass Lake Spearing Ban Evaluation," 1997).

More recently, Richard Hassinger, former chief of fisheries for Minnesota's DNR, put his finger squarely on the issue when asked whether spearing would be entirely banned (Grooms 1989):

> *That [darkhouse spearing] is less a management issue than a political issue, and it will be decided by the Legislature. Under the right circumstances, spearing provides additional recreation. But we think some waters should be managed for trophy fish, and that is incompatible with spearing.* (p. 22)

I take issue, however, with the notion that trophy fish management is incompatible with spearing for the reasons presented in this chapter. Spearing is incompatible with catch-and-release, but not "look-at-and-don't-spear!"

Former Minnesota DNR fisheries chief, C.R. Burrows (Fellegy 1974 p. 6), "...believes that spearing presents no real danger to northern pike populations, ...and that to save northerns you could have someone else give up his sport — for example, eliminate trolling or shorten the angling season."

Illegal Spearing

A third issue, one not worth much discussion, is that illegal fish are taken by darkhouse spearers (see Chapter 7). While this may be true, and I do not condone it, I doubt if illegal activity is any more common for spearers than for any other type of fishing. A MN DNR conservation officer in northcentral Minnesota found about one in ten winter anglers was in violation of a law, most often fishing with too many lines.

Muskies, Inc., claims that muskie populations have declined through accidental, but illegal, spearing (Swenson 1986). While the DNR claims "There's no factual evidence to show spearing harms northerns or muskies, ..." (Swenson 1986). The publicity surrounding the spearing of just one muskie has done a great deal of harm to the sport. However, illegal spearing in smaller lakes could impact muskie populations. On the other hand, muskies are very inactive in winter, which lessens the chances of illegal spearing.

A study of the attitudes of Minnesota's anglers found 58 percent of fishing club members thought prohibiting spearing was an effective way of protecting large pike (Baltezore and Leitch 1987). Only three percent of MN DNR personnel agreed. The study also showed that fishing club members thought they knew more about fisheries management than the DNR professionals.

Competition between muskie and northern populations is also a concern for fishery managers. Northern pike eggs hatch two weeks earlier than muskie eggs. When northerns are introduced into muskie waters, the population of muskies declines (Meyer 1991). If this is the case, muskie enthusiasts should be encouraging spearing of northerns. However, once populations stabilize, or where both occur naturally, them seem to get along OK.

Conclusions

Three of the four arguments against spearing — (1) it results in crippled fish, (2) spearers take the big fish, and (3) spearers take illegal fish — each have some foundation in truth. However, the consequences are either of no significant damage to the resource or are not just the result of spearing. Finally, the fourth argument — that spearing is not sport —is a value judgment and should be viewed as such.

My conclusions about spearing, as a critical believer in this case, are that neither the evidence nor the arguments definitively lead to a clear *for* or *against* position. I'll let you, the reader, draw your own conclusions.

Spearing is a legal way to take fish in Minnesota. Unless someone suddenly becomes capable of making acceptable judgments on the comparative value of different forms of recreational fishing, spearing is likely to remain a part of Minnesota's fishing tradition. (Sonnenburg undated)

A solution to the "spearers take bigger fish" part of the controversy is to do as many states and provinces have done with angling and limit the number of trophy fish kept. For example, all fishermen could be given (or sold) a limited number of trophy tags: two tags for northerns over 34 inches; five tags for fish between 29 and 34 inches, or one per day of this size; and so on. Bergh (1975) suggests treating spearing like big game hunting with two tags per season and let the spearer decide which two trophy fish to spear or keep when angling. Then it would be up to individuals how they chose to harvest their trophies.

Perhaps the winter [and summer] angler shouldn't be too hasty in persecuting the spearer, however. The spearer probably has more of an education about what is happening in the aquatic environment beneath his spearhole. He probably knows more about fish habits during the winter than most fishery scientists and certainly more than the ice fisherman who spends his time watching a bobber. (Fins & Feathers 1975)

Well, maybe this chapter wasn't so unbiased! But I think I laid out all the pertinent issues on both sides. The arguments used by opponents of spearing could be used against some of their own fishing methods, such as trolling, night fishing, fishing with live bait, or fishing with more than one line. At least the spearers aren't arguing to restrict anyone else's "sport." Until better information becomes available, let's each share the burden of saving some of the resource for tomorrow's sport fisherman.

Part II
Description

CHAPTER 4

Shelters

A variety of local names is used for the structure darkhouse spearers use depending on the location (see the chapters on individual states). Whatever the name — fishhouse, icehouse, shanty, shelter, hut, coop, darkhouse — the requirement is the same: a moveable structure that allows the spearer to see into the water while also keeping warm. The shelter is little more than an "enlarged water telescope" (Laude 1920). To the passerby, most look like outhouses scattered on the winter's ice.

A shelter is probably the most important component of a spearer's equipment. It may also be the largest and most expensive, especially if a stove is included. Houses are made of canvas, plywood, buffalo board, chipboard, sheet metal, aluminum, steel, fiberglass, black plastic, Tyvek, mobile homes, school buses, . . . and just about any other material the builder can gather together (Borge and Leitch 1988). There is no building code nor concern for aesthetics on the ice. Indians and trappers used to use make-shift darkhouses made from a blanket and snow blocks (Laude 1920).

A very adequate shelter can be put together using scrap materials for little more than the price of some new hardware. However, some spearers spend hundreds on their shelters. Even so, darkhouses do not even begin to rival the extravagances of shelters built by winter anglers (Stark and Berglund 1990).

Shelters can be purchased second hand at what sometimes seem to be high prices, until compared with the costs of materials. Many lumber yards and carpenters also build shelters for sale. There are also several fiberglass molded shelters available. The main drawback to commercially made shelters is that some of the character is lost, since home-built shelters are like snowflakes — no two are alike.

One Michigan shanty architect used 14 storm doors for the walls and roof, built on a chest freezer top for the floor (Griffin 1985). After spraying the inside with spray-foam insulation, it required very little to keep it warm.

I have built six shelters; the first in December 1963 was a 4x6-footer made of Masonite which turned out to be a bit on the heavy side. I sold that shelter in the late sixties.

My second shelter in 1965 was a very small 3x4½-foot canvas covered wood frame with barely room for one person. It couldn't have weighed more than 30 pounds. I can't recall what became of that shelter.

I built a deluxe 6x6 by 6½-foot high shelter in 1966 with paneling, wallpaper, and retractable wheels. It must have weighed 500 pounds, or more. Perhaps that was part of the reason it went through 5 inches of ice in December 1971 (see photo in Chapter 14). I sold it before the next season.

#1 4x6 Masonite

#2 3x4½ wood frame covered with canvas

#3 6x6 with wheels and heavy!

#4 3x5 made from scraps

My fourth shelter was a color-
ful 3x5-footer built in 1968 from plywood scraps from a neighbor's boat-
house that the shifting ice on Otter Tail
Lake had destroyed that spring. It blew
out of the back of my pickup once and
broke into its original pieces when it
hit the road. I gave that house to a
friend. He rebuilt it and used it for
several more years.

#5 4x6 plywood with a window

My dad used my fifth house
(4x6 feet), built from ¼" plywood in
1975, for a couple years, but he later
converted a 14-foot travel trailer to a
darkhouse, so my fifth house sits in
reserve. It was, however, the most
functional, being the perfect size,
lightweight, with room for one, or
maybe two, small visitors.

It has been 20 years since I built
my sixth darkhouse, a 3½ x5 foot portable. It had a plywood sand box bottom with plywood ends and canvas
sides that fold up. I sold that darkhouse for $25 at my parents' auction
sale in July 2000.

#6 3½x5 semi-portable

For the past couple of years I have speared exclusively from one of my two commercially made portable darkhouses. I bought an InsTent about the time the first printing of this book came out. It was the only manufactured darkhouse that could be shipped as baggage on commercial airlines and strapped to a Super Cub with skis and flown to a remote lake. About two winters ago I bought a Pop-N-Fish, that is a little bigger than the InsTent and weighs about half as much. The InsTent has a sewn-in floor, which helps to hold it down in the wind. I'm now considering one of the many sled-based portables (e.g., Otter, Fish Trap) that could be pulled behind my ATV.

Weight, warmth, and darkness are the primary considerations in shelter construction. Shelters are frequently pulled by hand onto early, thin ice, moved around by hand, and pulled off by hand in the spring. Thus, the need to be lightweight. However, weight is often sacrificed for convenience. Dad's travel trailer fishhouse is heavy, but extremely comfortable. My third house with wheels was very easy to move from lake to lake. Wheels are handy when they work, but frustrating when it's time to move and everything is frozen solid, the temperature is 30 below, and the wind is blowing 40 miles per hour.

Weight is also a consideration for stability when the winter winds blow across the ice. Lightweight darkhouses can be blown for miles across the lake if they are not frozen down or otherwise secured. Some people use one or more short ropes tied to the house and frozen into holes in the ice. I saw dozens of spearing and angling houses blown miles across Leech lake (Minnesota's fifth largest lake) after a strong wind in January 1990.

It needs to be warm in a darkhouse for two reasons. First, to keep the spearer warm. Spearers are not sissies; they just like to be comfortable. And,

#7 5½x5½ fabric InsTent

#8 6x6 fabric Pop-N-Fish

second, to keep the spearing hole free of ice crystals. Just a few ice crystals on the hole makes it difficult to see into the water.

Darkness is, of course, what gives the darkhouse its name. It must be dark so the spearer can see into the water and so light doesn't spook the fish. Rays of light penetrating through missed-nail holes or cracks in the walls can glare on the water and spook fish. I'm not sure of how much of a problem this actually is, but spearers will go to all lengths to plug up every hole. On the other hand, fish sometimes come in when the door is open.

Burlap sacks are sometimes used to block the light that might get in around the stove pipe hole, which has led to more than a few fishhouse fires.

One danger in making the shelter too dark or too airtight is that it could lead to asphyxiation. Many winter anglers and spearers are overcome each year by carbon monoxide poisoning when their stoves are not properly vented. A way to avoid this is to drink plenty of coffee so you have to open the door often.

Shelter dimensions. Darkhouses need to be big enough to accommodate the spearer, a stove, and at least a 2x2-foot spearing hole. While floor dimensions and designs vary considerably, most darkhouses have a six foot ceiling. I have seen and used houses with lower ceilings, some only four feet, but they are not very comfortable. Larger houses are more comfortable, but are also more difficult to move around.

The most common size of darkhouses is 4x6 feet (Borge and Leitch 1988), simply because many building materials come in 4x8-foot sizes and most full-size pickup boxes are slightly over 4 feet wide. Spearing is usually a solitary sport, so shelters do not need to accommodate more than one person. But, it is also nice to have room for visitors. I enjoy watching my wife or others spear more than doing it myself. Having an extra person in the shelter also provides an added pair of eyes to see another direction under the ice.

Some shelters are 4x8 feet with spearing holes in each end; others are 6x6 with 2x6-foot holes. Not all shelters are rectangular. I saw one that was cylindrical, made of thin steel. I always wondered how the occupant found enough corners to keep equipment in.

Occasionally a crafty darkhouse architect will add a piece to the side of the shelter to accommodate the stove or a larger hole. A rental shanty I used in Michigan had a tin addition on the back of shanty to house the heater.

Ice fishing shelters come in all shapes, sizes, colors, and materials.

Darkhouse openings. A shelter needs a door, a spearing hole, and a hole for the stove pipe. The stove pipe hole can be in the roof or the side and needs to be caulked up well so no light sneaks in.

The door should be just big enough for easy entry and exit, yet not too big so as to minimize the chance of light getting in. Jackets, rugs, blankets, and gunny sacks are often hung by the door to cover the cracks. Doors cannot be latched or locked from the inside in most states, so another type of catch or spring is needed to keep them closed.

Unfortunately, darkhouses are attractive places to loot for the likelihood of stealing a spear, antique decoys, fishing equipment, or a good stove. Each winter hundreds of shelters get broken into. For this reason, a strong door with a good padlock is necessary. Winter often makes it difficult to open padlocks with keys, so combination locks are sometimes used (with the combination written somewhere on the outside of the shelter, since fishermen have poor memories).

The spearing hole can be as small as 2 feet square to as big as 2x6 feet, or bigger. It needs to be large enough to see as much of the lake as desired, yet not so large that it is both difficult to cut and to keep open. Minnesota spearers reported holes from 18" by 18" to 3' by 5½', with 2x2 and 2x3 by far the most common.

I like a spearing hole of about 2x3 or 2x4 feet. That is one advantage of the Pop-N-Fish portable, I can cut a hole about any size I want, as long as I leave room for my chair. Larger holes are nice, especially when the fish are not decoying in very close, but they are difficult to cut in thick ice, more work to keep open, and more of a safety hazard when the house is moved away.

Floor plans. Just where to put the hole in the shelter floor is most important. One of the most challenging aspects of building a darkhouse is the floor layout. Spearing hole location considerations include where the door is, where the stove is, how many people the shelter will accommodate, and how the floor is constructed. If there are runners under the house, this may leave a 3 or 4 inch opening between the floor and the ice that needs to be plugged up to keep light, wind, and snow out. Snow and ice chips work best, but old rugs, carpet pieces, and cardboard also work well. But be sure to take this stuff along with you when you leave — don't litter.

Everything should be handy while you're sitting in the chair peering into the lake, so the interior layout is important. There should be enough nails and hooks to hang parkas, gloves, the ice skimmer, and other gear.

The area directly around the hole is very important. Decoys need to be hung in the hole just right, need to be easy to move around, and need to be reeled in at quitting time. Sticks, pairs of nails, open-faced casting reels, and short fishing rods can all be used to hang the decoy.

A nail or two may be necessary to prop the spear against so it is ready. I have even seen a mechanical device to hold the spear in a ready position. However, this may make too much noise.

A requirement in most states it to have the name and address of the owner painted on the outside of the house. Minnesota requires 3-inch high letters, while Alaska requires 12-inch high letters so they can be read from an airplane. Some use the premade stick-on numbers, others paint numbers on freehand with a brush or spray paint, some cut numbers from old auto license plates, and others do a professional job. Minnesota allows drivers license numbers to be used in place of your name if you are concerned about the paparazzi. I have nothing to worry about in that regard.

Typical darkhouse floor plans.

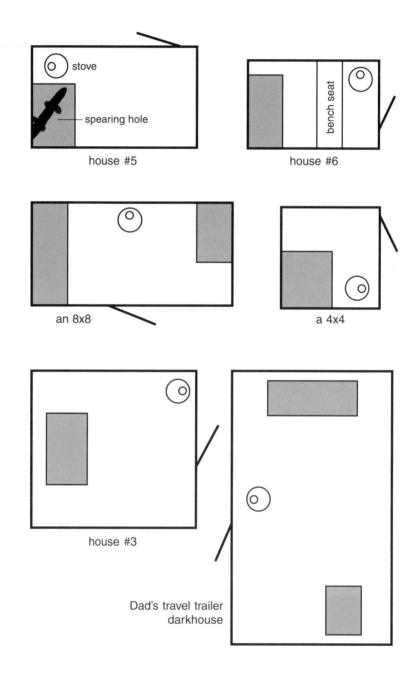

stove

spearing hole

house #5

bench seat

house #6

an 8x8

a 4x4

house #3

Dad's travel trailer
darkhouse

Colors. Imagination and creativity run wild when darkhouse exteriors are painted, while many remain unpainted. The outside can be a dark color to soak up the sun's rays and so it can be easily seen on the winter snow.

Darkhouse interiors should be dark. Yet some folks prefer a lighter interior so it is easier to see while they are inside the house.

Outsides are painted every color of the rainbow and some others. I usually just mix up enough left over paint to do the trick. I have seen houses painted like barber poles, polka dotted, with scenes, like Coke cans, and unpainted. Fish, of course, couldn't care less what color the house is.

Heaters

Shelter heaters are about as varied as shelters themselves. Some are homemade, but most are factory-made. Kerosene, propane, or wood are used in 99 percent of all darkhouses. Some will use electricity, if close enough to shore or from a portable generator. Solar power has even been used, but this is not very successful in the north's short days with the sun low on the horizon. Although, a dark-colored house really warms up on a sunny late January day.

Wood stoves. Wood was undoubtedly the first fuel used and is still used by many (36 percent in Minnesota), especially in areas where wood can be picked up along the shore. A darkhouse heated with wood is certainly the best smelling and seems quite comfortable. The problems with wood are obvious: wood to carry in, ashes to dispose of, and difficult control of fires.

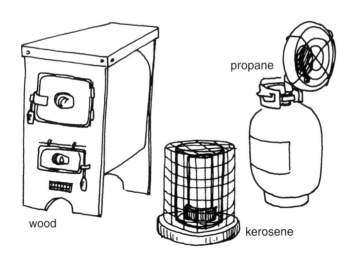

propane

wood

kerosene

Darkhouse heaters.

A friend of mine stepped out of his portable canvas house to get a breath of fresh air, only to turn around to see the house going up in flames. Apparently, something had been too close to the hot wood stove and the movement of opening the door was enough to get the flames going. Not willing to give up on his stove, he built another portable fishhouse, this time made out of chipboard panels fastened with screen door hooks. He and I left his house one evening in a whiteout, only to return the next morning to find it too had burned to the floor. The wood stove had struck again, but this time it had been hot enough to, fortunately, destroy the stove.

Kerosene or fuel oil was probably the next fuel commonly used in darkhouses. Kerosene stoves were very popular when I started spearing and the price of kerosene was low. However, only 13 percent of darkhouse spearers use fuel oil today. About the only advantage of kerosene stoves is the availability of fuel and its convenience.

Kerosene stoves have a number of drawbacks. First is that they soot up when burned at low temperatures. I had one stove that needed to be taken apart about every third day to clean it out. The alternative was to fire it up and blast the soot out, but this left a telltale plume of soot on the ice and snow around the house.

Another drawback is that kerosene stoves often get fired up too high because they are so difficult to get started. By the time a fire gets going there is a pool of fuel in the stove. Once it gets going, the stove and the stovepipe half way to the ceiling get red hot.

The other drawback is the occasional spill of kerosene that, almost without fail, ends up on the water in the hole making it difficult to see. It is then time to either move the house or let the hole freeze over and try to wipe up the kerosene with a rag.

My first 10 years of spearing were in a darkhouse heated with kerosene. The smell of fuel oil, kerosene, or diesel fuel still reminds me of sitting in a warm fishhouse. There is no smell quite like that of the inside of a damp darkhouse heated to 85 degrees. Even the exhaust from an occasional diesel-powered city bus or an 18-wheeler can bring fond memories of the darkhouse.

Propane is by far the most popular fuel in darkhouse today, with over half of Minnesota's darkhouse spearers using propane stoves. In October, a good propane fish house stove is worth its weight in smoked salmon. Many people make their own propane stoves using burners from gas ranges or water heaters.

Propane is the most popular heat source.

A 20-pound propane bottle will cost about $10 and will last a week with the stove running continuously. Until recently the only choices in propane bottles were 20# or 100#, but today propane bottles come in many smaller sizes, such as 5 to 10 pounds, that are easier to carry around. Propane is clean and the flame is easy to regulate. Besides the slightly higher cost, the drawbacks of propane include the dangers if not vented properly and the likelihood of getting the stove or the bottle ripped off.

Another drawback is blowing the house up by not being able to strike a match after having turned the gas on. More than once did I fumble around with cold fingers trying to get a match lit while propane continued to fill the stove. When the match finally lights there is something of a mild explosion in the house.

Today I use one of the BIC-type mechanical matches to light a catalytic heater (Mr. Heater) mounted atop a 7- or 20-pound propane bottle. Some people call these "sunflower" heaters, because they look like a sunflower head. While I don't have a stove pipe or vent, the canvas shelters have considerably more area of vent than a 3-inch pipe would provide.

Insulation

Insulating a darkhouse adds warmth, weight, and cost. Where weight and/or cost is a consideration, insulation is not necessary due to the small volume of air space to be heated in a darkhouse. Many people have begun to insulate their darkhouses with the lightweight beadboard-type insulation.

Portability?

So far I've talked about size, shape, construction materials, and heaters. One other variation is portable vs. non-portable. Rigid non-portable houses usually belong to the 'locals' who do not have far to haul them and leave them out throughout the season. On the other hand, spearers from the city or even some locals will generally have portable shelters. Less than 10 percent of Minnesota spearers had portable houses in 1988. Today, I'm sure that has risen to at least 20 percent with the availability of manufactured, portable fish houses.

There is just as much architectural variation in portable design as with nonportables. Portable houses have the luxury of compactness and are usually lighter. (Although my buddy Les knows how to build heavy portable houses.) Portability makes them easy to transport, perhaps several together, and to pull on and off the lake.

One major drawback of using a portable shelter is the need to cut a new hole each time. This is easy in December when the ice is thin, but not so easy by the middle of January when the ice can be 30 inches thick or thicker. I often find an abandoned hole that isn't too old or frozen too deep and chop it out. Saves the time of finding a spot too.

Another shortcoming of portable houses is getting all the holes and cracks sealed up so they are both warm and dark. This is even more difficult when the shelter is put up and taken down often, which is yet another drawback — setting it up each time.

Having just the right hook, nail, or corner to put things is not as easy in a portable house as in a non-portable.

A final drawback of portable houses is that they almost never work the way they were designed to work. Sure, they work fine in the garage in September, but that ain't field conditions. The hinges, pins, thumb screws, and braces never work the same when its 20 degrees below zero, when they are caked with snow and ice, or when there is a 30 mph wind. A fairly new item on the ice fishing market is ice screws to help anchor fish houses in place.

The Perfect Darkhouse

The perfect darkhouse would be lightweight, inexpensive, easy to transport, have all the necessary conveniences, be easy to keep warm, and come with a hole already in the ice.

■

Probably no other group of sportsmen
spend so much time putting comfort in,
and taking labor out, of their sport
as do frostbite fishermen.
But one suspects, after seeing their work,
the fixin' and fussin's as fun as the fishin.'

Erwin A. Bauer

CHAPTER 5

Equipment

Darkhouse spearing equipment is an important part of the tradition. I will discuss in more detail the most important pieces of darkhouse equipment — the spear, the decoy, and the chisel — and in less detail the other paraphernalia used. Some interesting references about darkhouse equipment are Emmet (1938), Griffin (1985), Chiappetta (1966) Laude (1920), Wisner (1983), Brazier (1985), and, of course, the Kimballs' books on decoys (1986, 1987).

Darkhouse spearing equipment is simple, yet it must be functional. Unlike open water fishing gear, spearing equipment has changed very little over the years. Commercial decoys are made of plastic, the stoves are much better, and the houses are of lighter material and more portable, yet nothing as high-tech as electronic reels, underwater video fish locators, or downriggers has found its way into the darkhouse spearer's gear.

Cutting the Hole

Spearers face a much bigger challenge cutting holes through the ice than do wintertime anglers who can simply auger a 6- or 8-inch hole through the ice. Spearing holes can be cut with an ice saw, chain saw, power auger, ice chisel, or ax.

Ice saws were more common in the earlier days of ice boxes. Today, ice saws are more antiques than functional. However, LeRoy Neulieb of Rothsay, Minnesota, and a few others, are again making ice saws. I bought one of LeRoy's saws at the start of the '90-'91 season and found it to work extremely well. LeRoy sharpened it for me once a couple years ago. Now, ten years later, it is a little bent here and there, but it still works just great.

A Neulieb ice saw at work.

To use an ice saw, a hole must first be cut in the ice using a chisel or an auger. Then three sides of the hole are cut with the ice saw and the fourth side is chopped with an ice chisel. Without a chisel or ax, the fourth side must also be sawed.

These saws cut through ice like a hot knife through butter, at least until the ice gets real thick. After it is about 15 inches thick I usually use the power auger to bore eight or ten holes, then cut between the holes with the saw. It takes me about ten minutes to cut a hole, even in 30-inch thick ice.

LeRoy Neulieb's ice saws, ice tongs, and other spearing equipment are available from Lakeland General Store in Dunvilla, Minnesota.

Ice saw prices in 2001.

Chain saw. Some darkhouse spearers use chain saws (31 percent in Minnesota) to cut the hole. While this is quick and easy — once the saw is running! — chain saws have some drawbacks. First is getting them started in the cold weather; the newer ones start pretty good. Second is lugging them along, yet they are no bulkier than power ice augers. Finally, oil from the chain may get into the hole causing the same problem as when kerosene is spilled.

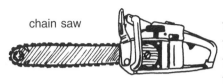

chain saw

The chain saws that ice sculptors use have a special ice chain. I've never used or even seen one, but it would be worth checking out for cutting a hole in the lake.

Power augers came on the ice fishing scene almost 40 years ago. Today's power augers are lightweight (around 30 pounds) and easy to start in the coldest weather. Over 20 percent of Minnesota's spearers use power augers. Most are gas powered, but there are some electric augers powered by the vehicle's battery or from the ATV 12V outlet.

I almost always use a power auger to cut spearing holes when the ice gets thick, unless I am somewhere remote where the weight and bulk are a factor. In fact, I've cut several spearing-sized holes through thick ice in one day to find just the right spot for Dad's darkhouse.

Eight or ten holes bored with an 8- or 10-inch power auger can open a large spearing hole in a few minutes. All that is left is to chop out the area between the holes with a chisel, or cut it with an ice saw. This leaves a jagged edge on the hole, but that can be shaved off with the chisel.

A power auger is used to cut spearing holes.

Eight to ten holes are bored in the ice.

The area between the holes is chopped away to open a large spearing hole.

Power augers and chain saws are both noisy, which may bother nearby anglers. But the noise doesn't seem to bother the fish and it is much quicker than chopping with a chisel. While fishing at about 10 am Christmas Eve 2000, the neighbor was boring his hole out when a 38-inch, 14# northern grabbed my artificial tullibee decoy. We baked him (the northern) later in the week!

Ice chisels, or "spuds," are more a part of the darkhouse heritage (Emmett 1938) than power augers or ice saws and are still used by most of Minnesota's spearers. Chisels serve a variety of purposes including cutting the hole, straightening out the edges when the hole has been cut with an auger, prying a house loose, and chopping the house loose after it has frozen in.

Chisels can be bought in sporting goods stores, from blacksmiths, or be homemade, and can be found in many variations. A simple, one-piece chisel can be bought for as little as $15, while a custom-made chisel can set you back $40 or more.

Weight and cutting edge are important characteristics of good chisels. A chisel should be heavy enough to cut well, but not so heavy that you can't chop for more than a few minutes. Ten or twelve pounds is about right for a 5-foot long chisel. A sharp chisel is all that is needed to cut a hole in just minutes in thin ice, even the 6-foot long holes. A sharp chisel will cut through 4 inches of ice with a single stroke.

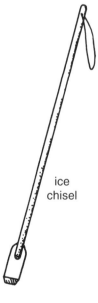

ice chisel

The business end of a chisel is usually hardened steel, to hold a cutting edge. Cutting edges come in a variety of flat, angled, or toothed styles. I have found a forked style to work the best.

Ice chisels need a ring or hole in the handle to run a short piece of rope through to put around your wrist, since it is surprisingly easy to drop one through the ice. A 12-pound chisel can get away really easy when you're chopping through thick ice and don't realize there's only ½ inch to go. The momentum drives the chisel right out of your hand.

I took a native Californian darkhouse fishing in Minnesota. Even after a warning about how easy it was to drop the chisel, he put it through the ice after about 10 chops. I don't usually have a rope on my chisels! I managed to finish the hole with a hatchet. I expected to see the chisel lying on the bottom, since it was only about 9 feet deep and crystal clear, but the bottom was very silty and there wasn't a trace of the chisel.

The lost chisel was the heaviest I had ever had, weighing perhaps 15 pounds. I was somewhat glad he lost it, especially since I get a great deal of pleasure from reminding him of it. However, I lost the replacement chisel driving off Otter Tail Lake in the winter of 1998-99. I hope whoever found it is still using it.

Not 100 feet from where that chisel was lost through the ice, my uncle lost the bottom half of a two piece chisel nearly 20 years earlier. Upon learning of this mishap, Jake moved his darkhouse over the spot in nearly 20 feet deep. Again, no sign of the chisel. He welded a small funnel on the female (upper) half of the chisel and somehow was able to screw it on the lost half and retrieve it. My uncle got that same chisel for Christmas two years in a row.

Ax. An ax works well for cutting holes (Laude 1920) when the ice is thick enough so the water doesn't splash and not over a foot and a half thick. A sharp double bit ax will cut a hole through 10 inches of ice in just minutes. Clean up can then be done with a chisel as well as a good chop on the fourth, uncut side.

Ice tongs. The larger chunks of ice can be removed from the hole using ice tongs, a shovel, or the chisel, or they can be broken into smaller pieces. Some even push the big piece under the ice, but this might get in the way of decoy lines or spook fish. I usually push the chunk under the ice if it is less than 6 or 8 inches thick. Any thicker than that and I pull it out with an ice tongs.

Skimmers. With the hole cleared of the big chunks, there are still the small chips to clear. What can't be scooped out with a shovel is skimmed by an ice scoop, skimmer, or sieve.

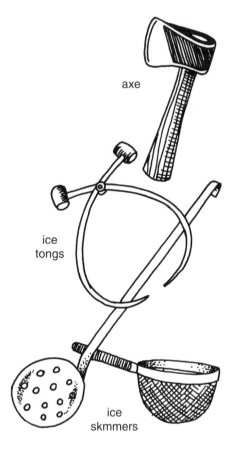

axe

ice tongs

ice skmmers

Ice skimmers for anglers are usually 4 or 5 inches in diameter. These are OK for small amounts of ice, but inadequate for cleaning out spearing holes. What seems to work better are french fry baskets from deep fryers or kettles with many holes drilled in them. However, even coffee cans with nail holes punched in them will work fine.

Spears

The spear is, of course, the rod-and-reel of the darkhouse fisherman. Next to decoys, spears are the most collectable of the paraphernalia used in the darkhouse.

History. Spears are the oldest form of fish capture device known, other than grabbing by hand. Spears were developed to extend the reach of the human arm. Fishing spears were developed in every corner of the world, in as many varieties (von Brandt 1964, Radcliffe 1921). Variations include material (from bone to steel), tine and barb design, number of tines, and type of handle. Modern spears evolved as modifications that improved both accuracy and fish-holding ability were found. Radcliffe notes (1921 p. 36):

> *The Spear-Harpoon stands out as the one fishing weapon whose existence is undeniable, whose employment is predominant. It is too world-wide and too well-known to need lengthy description.... The immediate successors of the single spear were probably the bident and trident. ...the broader surface of the trident helps to lessen the factor of error.*

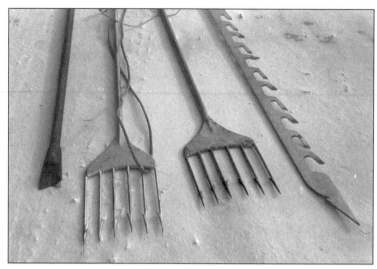

Seeba spears, Neuleib ice saw, and Cordes ice chisel.

Spears, or spear-like devices have a variety of names: spear, trident, harpoon, gig, plummet (a weighted spear head used in deep water in the Mediterranean, Norway and Japan [von Brandt 1964]), fish iron, and blowpipe (used in Thailand and South India for shooting fish).

Many early darkhouse spearers undoubtedly made their own spears, certainly the native peoples did, at least until iron spears were available in exchange for beaver in 1700s (Wheeler 1985). In 1932 *Popular Mechanics* magazine carried an article describing how to make a homemade spear from a broom handle, lead, and straightened sturgeon hooks ("Fishing Through the Ice").

However, even before 1900, commercially-made fish spears were available. Sears, Roebuck & Co. offered several spears in its mail-order catalogues around 1900 (Sears, Roebuck & Co. 1908). Wm. Mills & Sons, established as T.H. Bate & Co. in 1822, carried spears in its catalogues in the 1800s (William Mills & Son 1905).

A great coffee table reference book about fishing spears is *Ice Fishing Spears* by Marcel L. Salive (1993, MarJac Publications).

Contemporary spears. Sporting goods stores and bait shops usually carry five- or seven-tine manufactured spears. Prices run from about $20 to $50. I'm not much of a fan of these because the tines are thin, the barbs are weak, the handles are short, and they are just plain flimsy. The best spears are available from blacksmiths, at auction sales, or handed down over the generations. A good blacksmith-made spear, usually available in areas where spearing is popular, will cost $50 to $75.

Sturgeon spears, however, are neither flimsy nor inexpensive. They may weigh 25 to 35 pounds, have 8-foot handles with inch and a half diameters or more, and cost well over $100.

My idea of the ideal darkhouse spear for northerns is one with five tines, a 6-foot handle, and just enough weight so it goes straight. The 6-foot handle lets me get the spear in the water far enough so the refraction doesn't affect my aim. It also allows me to spear northerns without releasing the spear, since I usually run the decoy about 5 feet down.

A rope or line attaching the spear to the darkhouse, the chair, or your arm or leg is also necessary for the times the spear is let loose. The line should be at least 1½ times the length of the spear. While a small cord is really all that is necessary, I prefer a 3/8 inch rope because it is easier to find and hold onto.

One spear is really all that is needed, but some spearers have a standby in the darkhouse or the truck just in case they spear a fish in the tail and need a backup. In these cases it works best to let the fish go to the bottom, with the weight of the spear holding the fish down. Then, after both you and the fish have calmed down, deal a more accurate blow with the backup spear.

Just about dark one day in the winter of 1996, a northern slid through the hole near the bottom. I'm sure it was initially attracted by a decoy that my wife made and gave me as a present, and she was in the darkhouse watching. I speared it through the lips! I let it go to the bottom, where it just laid with its tail slowly moving back and forth. Now what?? I knew someone was in the house next door, so I asked Becky to go over and ask to borrow a spear. The person next door was the guy pictured on page 4 — what a coincidence! I used his spear to bring the fish out; it weighed 15 pounds.

I have only had three darkhouse spears in my 30 years of spearing. The first was a modified sucker spear that Jake gave to me. It is legal to spear spawning suckers when they run up creeks and rivers in early May in Minnesota. Such spearing, however, can quickly ruin a good darkhouse spear. That was the fate of my first spear after about its fifth season.

My second spear was a Christmas gift from my parents — one of those seven-tine, store-bought jobs. I used if for a couple winters and can't recall what became of it. I do remember putting a longer handle on it, only to have it leak and freeze, splitting the handle.

The spear I have been using for over 20 years was made by Cliff Seeba, Maine, Minnesota. He made spears for nearly 50 years. I paid $23 for that spear in 1974, bought another for a friend for $35 a couple years later, and paid $60 for another one in 1990. I still have those two "Seeba" spears.

Decoys

While some types of darkhouse spearing, such as for sturgeon, rely almost purely on chance, it takes something interesting to lure a northern into the hole. Aside from a few radical techniques (audio devices, for example) the two primary methods are live and artificial decoys. There are many good sources of information on artificial decoys, so I am not going to spend much time on them here.

Artificial decoys. Spearing decoys, or "fish" as they are called by collectors, have received more attention than any other piece of darkhouse equipment (Miller 1987, Breining 1994). They have become very much collectors' items (Kimballs 1986, 1987). As recently as 30 years ago, boxes of old spearing decoys could be bought at auctions and garage sales for just a few dollars. Today, even the poorest decoys bring high prices. I sold a dozen well worn, working decoys at an auction in July 2000 and received an average of about $40 each.

Frank Baron of Livonia, Michigan, has been publishing a list of collectable ice decoys since 1986. His seasonal list also contains sketches of decoys and short biographies of carvers. Frank lists both folk art and newer working decoys. The priciest "homemade" fish listed through the first 18 lists (through Winter 1990) were a 14-inch walleye by Hans Janner for $2600 (Baron 1986) and a 9-inch herring by Andy Trombley for $2000 (Baron 1990). The

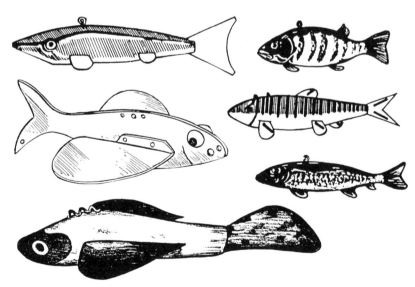

Various types of decoys.

Trombley was an old working fish, while the Janner was recently carved for the collector.

Baron's lists also contain commercial fish, those that are "factory made." A few commercial fishing tackle manufacturers made a few fish, but none for very long. These are among the rarest and most valuable. For example, a 3 1/5-inch fish by CCB Co., one of ten known to exist, was listed for $1500 (Baron 1986). Pflueger produced a few fish around the turn of the century. A 7-inch Pflueger from about 1900 was listed for $1000 (Baron 1990).

At least two companies have specialized solely in fish decoys — Randalls of Wilmar, Minnesota; and Bear Creek (now owned by K & K Tackle) of Hastings, Michigan. Randall fish are frequently seen on Baron's lists, with a 16-inch pickerel with $4.95 molded into its lead fin, listed for $250. I have a red-and-white one just like it among my many Randall decoys.

Decoy makers have imitated every fish found in fresh water and have even invented a few new ones. In addition to fish, there are turtle, duck, butterfly, mouse, crawdad, songbird, and snake lookalikes. Other odd designs include two-headed fish, fish eating other fish, fish painted on fish, schools of fish, mirrors on the sides of fish, and any possible combinations of spinners and flashers. While some fish are painted to look like the real thing, others are painted in all colors and designs from red and white to pink. Red and white is by far the most popular color (Bethel 1987).

Decoys are available in bait and sporting goods stores or from local carvers in some areas. Nearly every bait store in the areas that I fish has Duey's Decoys on display for sale. I met Duey Johnston, from New York Mills, Minnesota, shortly after the first printing of this book hit the streets. We swapped books for decoys. Duey and his wife, Nancy, have been making decoys for sale since 1989. They make at least three dozen different styles, varying in length, fish type, and coloration. Some are even filled with BBs so they rattle, others have spinners of other attractors connected to the tail fins. As far as I know, Duey only makes working decoys as do many other carvers; however, there may be just as many carvers that make decoys just for display.

Store-bought decoys are either plastic or wood, although I have also seen cast aluminum decoys.

Duey and Nancy Johnston in their New
York Mills decoy shop.

Duey Johnston with a 17-pound
northern he speared in December 1999;
was he using a Duey's Decoy?

The wood decoys have a carved body, usually with metal fins and
weighted with lead. The weight, fins, and eye-hook need to be placed just
right so the decoy swims when the string is pulled. The first homemade decoy
I made swam backwards.

Metal tails can be bent so the decoy swims either clockwise or counter-
clockwise. It is important to have some that swim each way so the decoy
string doesn't become twisted. It doesn't seem to matter how many swivels I
use, even with the pricier ball bearing swivels, the string gets twisted up after
jigging a decoy in the same direction for a while. Becky's favorite flourescent
orange decoy spun to the mucky bottom of Bass Lake (Underwood, Minnesota) when the eye hook came unscrewed — it is still there, but we bought a
replacement in 2000 for $9.95.

Plastic decoys are either solid with internal weights, or they are hollow
so they fill with water. Neither seem to swim quite as well as the carved
wooden decoys.

One characteristic that is universal among decoys is that they do not have fishhooks on them. Hooks are considered unsporting and are even illegal in most states. There are a few around with hooks on them, just the same.

Other types of artificial decoys and lures are also used. Sometimes a red and white Daredevil works well. I once used a flattened Pepsi can to attract a 5-pound northern. That was the first northern speared by my nephew, Danny.

Jigging sticks. Most decoys are designed to swim in a circle when jigged up and down. A "jigging stick" is used to get just the right motion. Some of these jigging sticks have even become collectors' items (Beskin 1951). Baron (1989) noted that

> *some of the most ingenious ideas ever devised by fishermen...were devised by ice spearing fishermen. Beside the conventional method of swimming the fish decoy, by manipulating it with a jigging stick, fishermen also use the method of twisting the line...a couple hundred times, and letting it unwind after being lowered into the water,..it unwound very slowly, giving a swimming effect. Another effective method was for the fisherman to tie his decoy tether line to one blade of an egg beater and slowly crank it, swimming the decoy in a circle at any desired swimming speed. The most unique method that I have heard of, was to tie a small fish decoy to a larger chub minnow or sucker, and let him tow the fish decoy as he swam around on his tethered line.*

Live decoys. State laws vary on what kinds of live fish may be used for decoys. Most common are suckers, perch, shiners, and chubs. It is legal to use perch in Michigan, but no longer legal in Minnesota.

Live sucker decoys can be bought in bait stores for about $1.50. They are usually from 8 to12 inches long, but can be over 15 inches long, depend-

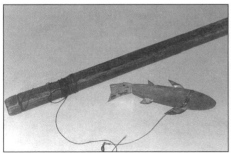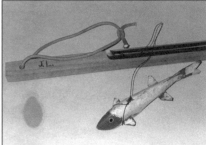

Jigging sticks.

depending on your preference. Northerns more readily grab the smaller ones and sometimes it only takes one grab to kill a decoy. However, the smaller decoys seem to live longer than the bigger ones. Rau's (1977) *Sports Illustrated* article chronicles the lives of "Herman" the sucker decoy.

Perch are abundant in most places where northerns are found. This made it easy to catch a decoy to replace a tired one when necessary (but, of course, that's not legal any more in Minnesota!).

Live decoys are presented in a variety of ways. Some people have even used live minnows in a jar (Baron 1989). I prefer a 10- or 12-inch noose made of 20# test braided line attached to a weighted leader. The amount of weight used depends on the size of decoy. I've only lost two decoys that way, and both of them in the winter of 2000-01. The first one was taken by a 6 pound northern that Becky said was too small to spear. The second one swam away after the slip knot gave way.

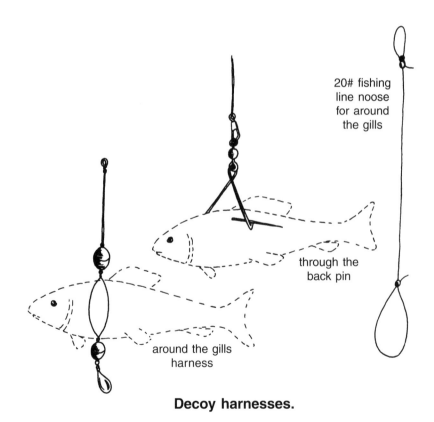

20# fishing line noose for around the gills

through the back pin

around the gills harness

Decoy harnesses.

Others use safety-pins through the back just forward of the dorsal fin. Chiappetta (1966 p. 137) explains that

> it [the decoy] should be carefully strung on a fine wire which is inserted just under the top fin but not through the vital spinal cord. This wire is then bent around and tied to the stout line.

He further notes (p. 137) that a good decoy "...may last through an entire season for the spearman." Obviously he is either very quick, has a very short season, or has never speared!

Lines attached to live decoys are wrapped around nails in the house wall, tied to jigging sticks, or attached to old reels (I suppose new reels would work too!). One advantage of using a reel is that it allows the fish to take some line out without breaking. I usually tie my jigging stick to a long piece of bungee cord strung along the roof over the hole — not having any nails in my portable houses. That gives it some slack in case something comes in and decides to make off with the decoy.

Miscellaneous Equipment

There are many other useful pieces of equipment that can be found in a darkhouse. The amount of extra gear usually depends on how early in the season it is, how portable the darkhouse is, and how large the darkhouse is.

Something to sit on. A chair with a good cushion is necessary for the many hours spent sitting watching down the hole. A back rest isn't necessary since you can't see down the hole when you're leaning back. Built-in benches, pails, and boxes also work for chairs. I've got a couple folding camp stools with zippered pouches beneath the seats. I keep spare matches and egg shells in the pouches.

Minnow bucket. A minnow bucket is needed to keep the extra decoys alive and to keep them overnight. The bucket is suspended into the hole two or three feet on a chain or wire, or it may be dropped to the lake bottom. Floating minnow buckets will not work, since they will freeze in the ice overnight.

Most bait stores now provide a plastic bag to carry the bait or decoys to the lake. They shoot a blast of oxygen into the bag to keep things alive.

A radio is useful for being aware of the weather and catching up on the top-40 or latest talk show controversy. Noises such as radios or talking do not bother fish, unless the radio is dropped on the floor.

A hammer, nails, and other hand tools are handy for repairs, adding nails in new places, and making adjustments to other equipment!

Coffee cans or ice cream buckets are useful to hold decoys and miscellaneous stuff. Even tackle boxes work well for this.

A flashlight comes in handy for finding things in the darkhouse. However, batteries tend to wear down fast in the very cold weather. Matches work well if you find what you're looking for quickly. Opening the door also works to provide some light.

Pails are used as makeshift chairs for visitors, for keeping live decoys in, for putting ice chips in, and for carrying the fish home.

A burlap sack is useful to carry fish home, to bank up the house when there isn't much snow, or to plug the area around the stovepipe hole.

A shovel is used to clear away snow when putting the darkhouse out, to bank the house up with snow, and to scoop ice chunks out of a newly cut hole. It also comes in handy when your vehicle gets stuck.

A knife is handy for cutting fishing line, slicing potatoes, or peeling apples.

Some angling equipment can be used to catch panfish when the northerns are not running or to entertain young visitors. Of course, angling while spearing is illegal in Minnesota.

A sled of some sort is handy to pull equipment to and from the house during early winter when the ice isn't safe to drive on. Sleds are also nice for hauling fish to shore.

Duct tape. Enough said. It doesn't stick too well when it is really cold, however.

Cell phones are handy to have along as long as they are turned off and only used to make outgoing calls — fishing is no place to be bothered with incoming calls!

Finally, **a coffee can** with a cover comes in really handy when you've had too much coffee to drink, when you have children along, or when it is inappropriate to go out behind the darkhouse. It sure beats making a special trip to shore.

Summary

Like most sports, the amount of equipment used and available usually greatly exceeds what is necessary. Spearing is no exception. A simple house, chisel, spear, ice skimmer, and a decoy or two will do just fine. But getting gear together is another way of extending the season.

CHAPTER 6

A Day in the Darkhouse

By now you should be starting to get an idea of what it is like to spear fish in a darkhouse, especially if you paged through and looked at the photos and drawings. However, there are many little things that happen that can add to the thrill, the work, or the passion for spearing. This chapter was written to introduce those nuances. The "day" described is chocked full of events, more than would happen during any one day of spearing. This imaginary day involves getting ready, getting to the spot, setting up or opening up, spearing, and going home.

A day of spearing as the Chippewa Indians did is described by the Kimballs (1986). The major difference is equipment, especially the Chippewa tent shanties on a framework of branches. Another difference is that some Chippewa tent shanties were made for laying down, not sitting.

Getting Ready

Getting ready sometimes means getting up early, which I have trouble doing. Fortunately, though, early for spearing is not the same as early for summer

All packed up and ready to go. Note house #7 strapped on top of house #6.

walleye fishing. When my Dad asks what time to expect me up in the morning, I always say, "We're getting up early to go fishing." To this he always replies, "I've heard that same song so many times before!"

The older one gets, the more enjoyment there seems to be in getting the gear ready for another season. This might be because we can now afford more gear, or because playing with the equipment is not as much work as actually using it. In some cases, assembling, readying, or even collecting the gear displaces the activity itself. This is the case with much open water fishing where the equipment has taken over the sport.

Getting ready involves gathering up the appropriate items of equipment described in the last chapter, trying to recall where they were put so they would be remembered. Things usually need to be fixed up or altered — put a new line on the decoy jigging stick, sharpen the chisel, patch the fishhouse, sew the chair cushion, . . . However, in my case, most fixing and alterations are forgotten about until the darkhouse is on the ice, and then it's too late.

Breakfast and a Fresh Decoy

Stopping for breakfast at a local eatery along the way is clearly part of the experience. A big plate of eggs, hashbrowns, with a side order of pancakes and several cups of coffee is a great way to start the day off right. After breakfast, it is time to stop in the local bait store and pick up a fresh sucker decoy or two. I know of at least one combined bait store-cafe, which makes it easy.

Big decoys were about $1.50 each in 2001.

Darlene Erickson bagging up a sucker decoy at Lakeland True Value, Dunvilla, Minnesota, January 2001. A shot of oxygen is added to keep the decoy fresh.

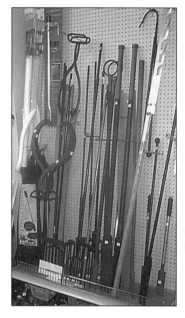

Spearing equipment for sale
at Lakeland True Value.

To the Spot

Many decisions need to be made about where to put the darkhouse: which lake, where on the lake, how deep, how close to other houses, which way to set it relative to the sun, and whether the ice is safe or not. If the ice is safe enough to drive on (see Chapter 14) that makes it easier than having to pull push, and drag the house to just the right spot. This is where portable houses are a blessing. Snowmobiles and ATVs are often used to pull fishhouses out onto the early-season ice

An ATV is handy when the ice is less than 8 inches thick, but at least 4 inches.

A DAY IN THE DARKHOUSE

Driving onto and on the lake are both experiences. There are fewer useable accesses to the lakes in winter, especially when the snow gets deep or has drifted. Also, as the ice gets thicker and the weather gets colder, it expands and pushes up on shore making it difficult to drive onto the lake. Someone else usually has the ambition to chop a track through the pushed up ice on shore and clear the path.

Snow on the lake can cause problems for getting around. The weight of the snow also adds weight on the ice, sometimes resulting in water on top of the ice. This condition is called "flooding" and makes it exciting to drive on the lake. Many fishhouses are frozen into the lake when there is flooding. It's darn hard work chopping one out with 4 or more inches of ice over the floor.

Even 2-foot thick ice will crack and groan when driven on. This really excites novice ice fishermen, but as Stark and Berglund (1990) point out in one of their stories about Mille Lacs Lake in Minnesota, driving on the lake is safe for those who are careful and know the lake.

A 6-foot ice push-up along shore.

Getting on the lake is usually easier on smaller lakes. This picture was taken from the lake, looking toward shore.

Finding just the right place to put the darkhouse is more important than finding a place to fish in open water. If you want to move in open water, its just a matter of pulling the anchor. With a darkhouse, moving involves cutting a new hole. Treat (1987) found that anglers without houses were more successful than those with houses, possibly because they were less reluctant to move. Some darkhouse spearers put their houses on the same spot every winter, probably no more than a few feet from where they were the winter before. This is easy on small lakes or close to shore, but a mile or two from shore on a large lake it is sometimes hard to find the same spot.

Contour maps can be a big help finding a spot if there are no other darkhouses on the lake. The right spot is usually 6- to 12-feet deep, preferably on or near a dropoff. There should be a weedbed nearby as cover for bait fish and habitat for northerns. Northerns are especially fond of cabbage weeds; the various broad-leafed members of the *Potamogeton* family (e.g., *P. Richardsonii* or *P. Praelongus*).

Many outdoor sports enthusiasts now use various GPS (global positioning system) technology to locate hot spots. I've found these aren't all that useful for fishing on lakes less than a couple thousand acres, since you can usually line up with a landmark or two along the shore quite easily. A point, a distinctive lake cabin, or a cell-phone tower, all make good landmarks.

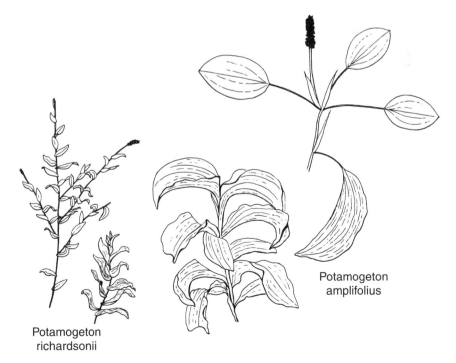

Potamogeton
amplifolius

Potamogeton
richardsonii

A DAY IN THE DARKHOUSE

Under some early ice conditions — when it freezes clear — you can walk on the ice and see the lake bottom just as clear as walking on air. In these cases it is really easy to find just the right spot. You might even see fish while walking on the ice. I have driven on lakes with a foot of clear, smooth ice; it's like flying really slow and low.

When other houses are on the lake already, they usually are in the best spots. This is a good indication of where the fish are, but you don't want to be too close to the others. In fact, Minnesota law prohibits anyone from placing a fishhouse within 10 feet of another fishhouse. Larger houses clumped together in bunches are more than likely angling houses, while smaller houses lined up along dropoffs are more apt to be darkhouses.

If the ice is too thick or cloudy to see through, there are no other houses around, and you are unfamiliar with the lake, it is time to cut some test holes to check the depth and the bottom. More than once I thought I knew what I was doing and cut a spearing-sized hole through thick ice and found out it was too shallow, too deep, or thick with weeds.

A test hole cut with the chisel or auger should be big enough to look through. Simply clear the ice chips out, put a blanket or parka over your head, and check the bottom out. If you can't see the bottom, it is either too deep, the water is murky, or the bottom is dark. Too deep means it's time to try to find a shallower spot. Murky water means go to another lake. Dark bottom means something may need to be put on the bottom to lighten it up.

Cutting a hole to test depth and weed conditions.

Looking into the test hole.

Setting Up

Before the hole is cut there is one more decision — which way to face the darkhouse. If the hole is square, it is easy to shift the house, but if it isn't, it's too late to change after the hole is cut. The question is, Should you watch toward the shallow side, toward the dropoff, or along the dropoff? Which way will the fish come from? Which way does the wind come from most often? The least airtight side of the house should face away from the wind. Finally, maybe the door should face the road or access so you can peak out now and then to check on the neighbors or see who is coming. The answer is simple, face the side of the house with the hole north, so it is out of direct sunlight. This prevents any bright spots or sun rays from shining in the hole.

Removing the large ice chunks with an ice tongs.

The last chapter described how to cut the hole. When there is no snow on the ice, the ice chips should be saved so they can be used to bank up around the house. Banking is necessary to keep the wind and light out. Burlap sacks and carpet scraps work

A fresh hole almost ready for use.

well too. The problem with sacks and carpet is that they freeze in and are hard to pull loose when it's time to move the house.

A hole needs to be cut using one or more of the tools described in the previous chapter. Then, slide the house over the hole, using the chisel to pry the house to just the precise placement. The first look down a freshly cut hole is always exciting. You never know exactly what to expect, except on some lakes where bottom conditions are fairly uniform. There might be a rock pile to the left, a tree branch to the right, some tall weeds straight ahead, and a rusting can right below.

I put my house on a hole someone had left a few days before and was surprised to see a Bear Creek decoy lying on the sand bottom next to a Swedish pimple. Both, I suspect, fell in the hole as the previous occupant moved the house off. It took me about 30 seconds to hook the pimple and 30 minutes to snare the decoy. But it paid off, I speared a 10-pound northern that day and added a decoy to my collection.

Who lost these in South Turtle Lake?

After taking a quick look down the fresh hole, it is time to clean the ice chips from the hole. When this is done, go back outside and bank up the places where the light is still shining through and bring the rest of your gear into the darkhouse. It'll take a few minutes for your eyes to adjust before you can see really well. The lake bottom might be hard to see because it is too deep, the bottom is covered with dark material, or because the ice is thick or covered with snow. On the other hand, the bottom might be so bright the whorled branches of muskgrass (*Chara vulgarish*), actually a macroscopic alga, can be seen on the bottom 10 feet below.

If the bottom is dark, drop some sliced potatoes, potato peelings, egg shells, white beans, or shelled corn to the bottom. Even though it is easy to see the decoy and fish without these, it is hard on the eyes to stare down a dark hole when you can't tell where the bottom is. Don't use too many spuds or egg shells; these are considered litter and it is illegal (but OK if done in moderation).

Opening Up

Now let's go back and start over as if the house were already on the lake or we were going to use someone else's house. The first thing to do is unlock the door, which may be hard if it's really cold and blowing. Next, get the heater going to warm things up. Then the hole needs to be cleaned out. If it was a mild night, the skimmer may be all that is needed. If it has been cold and you haven't been there for a couple days, the chisel is necessary. If the ice gets too thick (6 inches or more) it may be better to cut a new hole outside and move the house. There isn't a lot of room inside a darkhouse to be cutting through a foot of ice. The house tends to get full of ice chips if you do a lot of chopping.

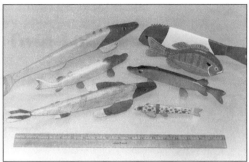

Some of the author's decoys.

It is good to have a selection of decoys to choose from. These were made by Duey Johnston.

A pail might be handy to haul the chips from the house. The bigger the pile of ice chips outside the door, the longer the house has been on the same spot. Blood on the ice can be a clue to how successful the spot has been, but many spearers keep their fish inside or hide them in their vehicles. They don't want anyone knowing what they're catching. Yellow ice is a clue to either how much coffee is drunk or how long the house is occupied at one time.

Live decoys are kept alive in sinking minnow pails hung into the hole on chain or wire propped away from the edge of the hole with a stick to keep the chain from freezing in. Chain or wire is used because there is a tendency to chop ropes off with the chisel. Minnow pails are kept inside one of the other pails in the house while fishing. Find a lively sucker from the pail, maybe the one from yesterday with the line already around its gills. Hang the decoy in the hole and turn the radio on. Check to see that the spear rope is not tangled and YOU'RE FISHING!

This is it! You're Spearing!

This is what you wait for, watching the decoy swim around, waiting for the big one to come in. Thoughts drift from what's happening in the hole to a hundred other things, but that's one advantage of fishing — it gives you time to think. Just when you least expect it, unless warned by a scared decoy or fleeing perch, a northern slides into view.

About the time you're comfortable, water starts dripping from the ceiling from condensation caused by the 85 degree heat inside the fishhouse the day before. Fifteen minutes of high heat with occasional wiping usually takes care of the dripping, but that often leads to melting ice on the floor that drips into the hole.

Other fish in the hole are one of the first things newcomers to the darkhouse notice, after they get over the fear of falling in the hole. Many other species swim through for a look around, some attracted by the decoy, others just going about their business. A bullhead used to come by a hole on South Turtle Lake just about every day at about the same time checking out her territory. Perch are plentiful in most northern lakes, providing relief decoys when the sucker plays out. Although, using perch for decoys has been illegal in Minnesota since 1978. Other visitors might include sunfish, crappies, walleye, eelpout, dogfish, whitefish, minnows, bass, carp, suckers, and bullheads.

Muskrats. Upon occasion there are forms of life other than fish that pass through the hole. My first experience with muskrats (*Ondantra zibethicus*) came when I was fishing near an inlet on Detroit Lakes (Minnesota). Muskrats went through the hole on a regular basis, but the one that came up to the surface really startled me. Muskrats even started a food cache in the house next to mine.

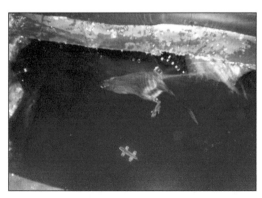

This muskrat came by about every 15 minutes on Leech Lake.

One spearer in Michigan's Lake St. Clair described his experience with a muskrat:

I was sitting in the shanty, staring down the hole, half-asleep, half-gassed from the heater when this monster came right up out of the hole, sat down and took over the shanty. I tried to unlock the door but couldn't. I took the door, hook and hinges with me. People out on the ice thought I had gone crazy. (Hacker 1989, p. 5B)

While the only warm-blooded animals I have seen swim through the hole were muskrats, it wouldn't surprise me if some spearers have seen beavers (*Castor canadenis*) go through the hole.

A common spearing story is the one about the black lab (Stark and Berglund 1990). Seems as how this lab jumped in the water after a fish in one darkhouse and came up in someone else's spearing hole! It is a story that gets around, whether it is fiction or not we may never know. Another version from the Fergus Falls (Minnesota) *Daily Journal* goes like this:

In the interest of public safety and out of concern for others, I would like to relate what happened to me last weekend. The rather balmy weather caused me to ignore the possibility of thin ice, and inspired me to take our dog Jake for a walk on Jewett Lake, which is near our home. Actually it is my husband's home during the ice fishing season. As we neared the lake, frisky Jake ran on ahead of me and must have come across some thin ice because suddenly there was a crackle and snap and down he plunged into the icy water. The splashdown must have disoriented him because he swam along the bottom for a ways until he came up in the hole of Dagmar Larson's spearing house. He and his brother-in-law, Arvid Svenson, (they married the Torvigg sisters, you know) were huddled in there fishing, playing cards and sipping whiskey. A little more of the latter, I think. There had just been some mention of unscrupulous card playing and it was really heating up in there when Jake roared up out of the water, upsetting the card table and scaring the daylights out of them, which prompted certain cards to appear from under Arvid's chair. Jake broke out the door, leaving the two men loudly discussing less than honest poker techniques.

All the commotion compelled Vernon Erickson in the fish house next door to get up from his lunch and investigate. As he leaned out the door, Jake, full of joy and celebration, bounded at him with great enthusiasm, knocking him down and upsetting the woodstove which started the fishhouse on fire.

Now Dagmar isn't speaking to Arvid and the Torvigg Christmas is just about ruined; Vernon's fishhouse is a pile of cinders and he won't be able to sit for a week; Jake's not quite thawed out and I think the fish have stopped biting. So please, if you're going to walk on thin ice, leave your dog at home.

> *Lois Reff*
> *Fergus Falls*

Ice cracking. Freezing ice makes a range of cacophonous and melodious sounds inside the darkhouse. The darkhouse serves as a megaphone, magnifying the sounds. Rau (1977) describes it as "groaning." The farther the thermometer is below zero, the more noise the ice makes as it freezes and shifts around. As the freezing ice expands, it cracks, pushes against itself and up onto shore, and creates pressure ridges. Being close to a pressure ridge is both a noisy and a "moving" experience. The ice can shift a few inches or a few feet, and water moves up and down in the hole.

People going by. When the ice is thin, people walking on the ice can be heard coming for a long distance. Once next to the house, their shadows can be seen on the lake bottom. Vehicles can be heard from a long distance,

A pressure ridge on Leech lake.

the ice cracking and popping. When they get too close to the house, it makes the water go up and down in the hole. The sound of someone chopping a hole can also be heard quite a distance away. I always hope the noise will drive the fish toward my house, but the fish probably don't even notice.

Visitors. While spearing is a solitary sport, spearers like to know how their neighbors are doing. Spearers in nearby houses come to check up on your luck. Sometimes they knock and talk from outside the house, other times they peer through the door just long enough so your eyes need to readjust and other times they come inside and watch down the hole for a while. Becky spotted a northern in the hole on our last spearing day in Minnesota during the 90/91 season, but my father had just driven up and was walking toward the door. She thought he would get to the door before she speared the fish, but she was wrong.

Coffee and snacks are necessary when sitting in the darkhouse for hours on end. However, coffee is a prime cause of yellow snow. I once put a can of pop on the ice under the floor. It slid into the hole just as a northern came in right along the bottom. Needless to say the northern took off as the can passed by his snout. I managed to snag the pop-top ring on my first try and retrieve the can.

Dropping things in the hole is common and a fear of many people, especially children. It is usually easy enough to retrieve things with a fishing line and also provides a little challenge. Sometimes the item is too heavy or just cannot be hooked. I have seen people put animal traps on the ends of poles to retrieve items from the lake bottom. I suppose magnets would work for some things. My dad speared his ice skimmer a few times to get it back from the lake bottom!

Sun shifts. As the sun moves across the winter sky, it causes cracks and holes in the house to appear as sun beams inside as well as dancing shadows in the hole. The leaks are patched with tape, gum, tarp or a coat in front of the hole. The canvas on my portable house #6 got so worn that I had to put an army shelter-half over the top to minimize the light. One day I had to chase the shelter-half across South Turtle Lake when it got away from me in the wind. I bought new fabric for my portable house soon after that.

Jigging the decoy keeps things happening in the hole and keeps the spearer awake. Some people jig their decoy nearly constantly, while others jig a little, then let the decoy sit still for a few minutes. Live decoys also need occasional encouragement to keep them swimming. When jigging the decoy isn't enough to attract a fish or to keep things interesting, putting another decoy on sometimes helps. Although it doesn't really seem to matter what is hanging in the hole, it is fun to keep trying different styles and colors.

Teasing a small one can be a way to learn more about fish habits and your will power. I mention in the Alaska chapter about teasing small northerns up into the hole. Other fish, like walleyes, bass, and eelpout, can also be teased and kept in the hole. I once kept a small walleye, maybe a pound, around the hole until a 15-pound northern came through and took it. The northern never slowed down; neither did my pulse for a while.

Spear a fish! When the perch or other fish leave the hole in a hurry, all in the same direction, and the live decoy comes to life and tries to leave the hole, it is time to get ready because a northern is not far behind. This is when my heart starts to pound, always expecting it to be the big one.

Sometimes it's just a little northern, a walleye, or an eelpout. Sometimes nothing comes into view and the perch come back. Other times a northern will lazily swim in, stare at the decoy for minutes, and just as lazily leave. Most exciting is when they charge in like a streak and either hit the decoy, miss it and turn around for another try, or hit/miss and leave.

When northerns get a taste of an artificial decoy, they will usually shake their head and head out of the hole in a hurry — they seldom return. However, when they miss it, they often come right back in the hole and try again. When they hit the live decoy and take it out under the ice, they can often be pulled back in, or, if they drop the decoy, they usually come back looking for it. All of this usually happens in just seconds, but it is the seconds that make all the work and waiting worthwhile.

When northerns come into view before making a hit, their eyes are fixed on their prey. Then, just before they strike, their body kinks into an S-shape to give them a quick shot at the decoy.

Spearing fish in six or more feet of water isn't as easy as it may seem. Refraction makes fish appear where they aren't, makes the spear appear to bend where it meets the water, and often causes the novice spearer to miss the target. (Actually, refraction happens when a ray of light passes from one medium to another, it changes direction in such a way that the sine of the angle of incidence divided by the sine of the angle of refraction is a constant characteristic of the pair of media (Chalmers 1982).) Dad insists he has a spear that won't go straight!

I generally put my spear at least half way into the water and watch the spear head and the fish, ignoring the "bend" in the spear handle at the water-line. Then, with a short jab, the spear hits its mark right behind the northern's head.

A 4-pounder, right behind the gills!

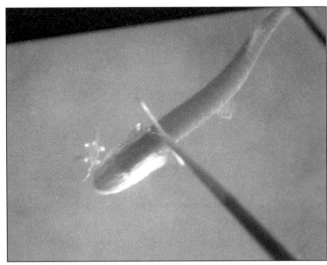

I took one of my colleagues, from North Dakota, spearing on Otter Tail Lake for his first time. After I showed him how to spear the first one, he assured me he could do it. Three clean misses later, he gave up. It just takes practice.

A large northern will provide quite a bit of action, even on the business end of a spear, except for the times when a spear tine hits the backbone. Once on the spear, they are not always easy to get off. I usually just open the door and give the spear a jerk. The fish will flop a few times and then be sharp frozen.

If you get excited and a spear tine hits the floor or the ice, or you bump the wall, most of the time the northern will leave in a flash, but not always. Sound travels almost five times faster in water (1400 to 1550 meters per second) than in air (330 to 340 meters per second).

Sometimes when spearing over a lake bottom that is silty rather than sandy, clouds of silt billow up when the speared fish thrashes on the bottom. Often, puffs of silt are left behind from perch making a hasty retreat. Some spearers will tie their spears up short so they do not quite hit the bottom. Others believe that stirring up the bottom muck attracts fish. While I don't intentionally stir up the bottom, I doubt if it is detrimental to fishing. It does seem to attract smaller fish, which may also attract the attention of northerns.

The urge to move gets pretty strong when there hasn't been any action for a while. However, moving a darkhouse involves more than just boring another hole in the ice or pulling up the anchor. Usually a short walk outside or a visit to a neighboring house will dispel any urges to move the house. If you do decide to move, be sure to clean up around the house. Push the ice chunks back into the hole. Some people put a stick in the hole to warn others and keep them from falling or driving into the hole until it has chance to freeze over.

Becky with a 6-pounder from East Twin Lake, Alaska.

Ice may start to form in the hole if it is really cold or if there are cracks for the wind to blow through. This is annoying and makes it more difficult to see into the water. I usually just push the ice to one side with a decoy tail or the jigging stick until there is enough to scoop up with the skimmer; then I scoop it out and put it in the minnow pail or throw it out the door.

Water bugs. There seems to be life everywhere in a darkhouse hole even though the water is near freezing. There are tiny waterfleas (Copepods), almost too small to see, that dart around an eighth of an inch at a time. There are backswimmers or water-boatmen (Notonecta sp.) that come up into the hole for air. Occasionally a giant water bug (*Hemiptera lethocerus ambrysus*) or a water scorpion (*Hemiptera rantra*) comes by for a look around. At least there are no mosquitos.

Snowmobiles. I once had my darkhouse on Battle Lake (Otter Tail County, Minnesota), which has been closed to spearing since 1967. It is an experimental lake — muskies were planted in it. The town of Battle Lake is along the lake shore. It seemed like the snowmobilers would use my fishhouse as one of their trail markers. They sometimes get annoying.

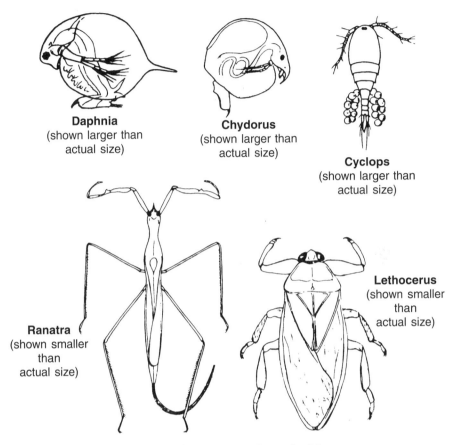

Daphnia
(shown larger than
actual size)

Chydorus
(shown larger than
actual size)

Cyclops
(shown larger than
actual size)

Lethocerus
(shown smaller
than
actual size)

Ranatra
(shown smaller
than
actual size)

Various water bugs seen in a darkhouse.

Other animals sometimes come around the ice.. There are usually some crows out picking on the minnows and rough fish left on the ice by anglers. I saw a whitetail deer on the ice once, probably spooked by some dogs. My brother-in-law's black lab, Duke, came by for a visit and took a leak on the corner of my house. The water in the hole turned a bright yellow! I moved the house.

Looking outside every once in a while is a good idea. It is easy to lose track of the weather and the time from inside a darkhouse. I was once trapped in a blizzard on Otter Tail Lake. My buddy's car wouldn't start so we had to

Leech Lake northerns, from 3 to 6 pounds.

walk off the lake. We knew which way the house was facing and there was a strong north wind, so we just walked to the north shore. The next morning Bob's house was gone, it had burned down (see the wood stove story in Chapter 5).

Quitting time. Since **the big fish** is always just about to come, it is hard to quit, unless there hasn't been any action all day. When I go out in the afternoon, I usually fish until it is too dark to see, or until I start seeing things in the hole that aren't really there. Then it is time to put things away and head for home. Most darkhouse spearers get to their houses by 8 or 9 a.m. and leave by 1 p.m. This seems to be the prime time for northern movement. However, that may simply be because that is the prime time for spearers to be in their houses.

Be sure to clean up around the darkhouse before leaving. Pick up any litter and push the ice chunks into the hole. It is common practice in Minnesota to put a branch in the hole to warn others. However, the hole freezes over enough to walk on or drive a snowmobile over in just one cold night.

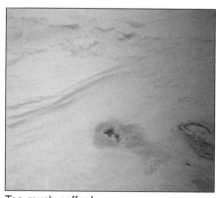

Too much coffee!

Be considerate of others when leaving a big hole in the ice.

Heading Home

The drive home starts with the anticipation of whether or not the pickup, sitting in subzero temperatures for several hours, will start. Then it's getting off the lake. Once home there are fish to be cleaned and eaten. Northerns are easy to clean, and contrary to popular belief, they are the best tasting fish in the lake.

Cleaning northerns has always been an exciting part of the spearing experience. Although, I'll have to admit that Dad usually ends up cleaning the fish — he likes to. What's exciting is discovering what the fish have in their stomachs. Half the time in winter, their stomachs are empty. I have found minnows, perch, sunfish, crappies, and many unidentifiable remains in the stomachs of northerns. We have even taken several northerns from South Turtle Lake with live frogs in them — in winter.

Darkhouse spearing is just one of those activities where you must be there to fully appreciate it. Try it and see for yourself. Get acquainted with a darkhouse spearer; they usually have an extra pail for visitors to sit on.

A DAY IN THE DARKHOUSE

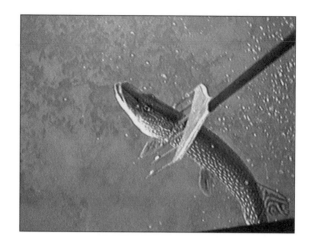

Part III
State Summaries

CHAPTER 7
Minnesota

Darkhouse spearing of northern pike has been a popular winter sport in Minnesota for at least 75 years. Spearer numbers peaked at nearly 65,000 in 1955, but currently only about 20,000 Minnesotans purchase spearing licenses each year. Annual license sales decline following price increases and in seasons with poor ice conditions. Over 100,000 shelter licenses have been sold each year since 1985, with the exception of 1996 when only 94,980 were sold because of deep snow. As of the day I am writing this (January 20), it looks like a record number of shelter licenses will be sold this season (2000-01) in Minnesota. This is thanks to a great winter for ice fishing and the increasing numbers of commercially-made portable shelters available. Another 1100, or so, rental shelter licenses are sold each year as well.

Spearing requires an angling license, a darkhouse spearing license, and a darkhouse license (Minnesota Department of Natural Resources at www.dnr.state.mn.us). The spearing license merely legitimizes the method; still only three northerns may be taken per day by spear and hook-and-line combined. Charging an extra fee for spearing goes against the opinions of a majority of Minnesota anglers. When asked "should [DNR] charge special fees on certain waters and for certain types of fishing?" almost two-thirds of the several thousand surveyed disagreed, with 30 percent strongly disagreeing. Only 21 percent agreed with the statement (Leitch and Baltezore 1987). However, requiring a special license makes it much easier to monitor participation.

Non-residents are not allowed to spear in Minnesota, nor are they allowed to license fishhouses, except for portables.

Only northern pike, catfish, whitefish, and rough fish may be speared through the ice from December 1 to February 15. Rough fish may also be speared in open water starting May 1st.

Darkhouses and other shelters must display the owner's name in 3-inch high letters. "A metal tag, furnished with the license, must be attached to the exterior side of the door, not more than six inches below the top of the door."

(Minnesota DNR 1991). The shape of the metal tag is changed each year so conservation officers can readily check whether they are current or not. It's not that the wardens can't read, it's just that shape is easier for them to see from a distance. The MN DNR introduced electronic licensing in 2000 and the tag is now printed on the vendor's printer on a self-stick label. I just stuck the new labels to the old tag.

Darkhouse doors may not be locked from the inside, maybe because angling is not permitted in a darkhouse as long as there is a spear in the house. At least twice Minnesota conservation officers have zipped up the door on my portable before I knew they were there! The first thing one of them said was "Oh, I read your book; how's your dad doing?" Also, fishhouses may not be placed nearer than ten feet from an existing house.

Northern Pike

Northern pike can be speared in almost all of Minnesota's 4,000 or more lakes with northerns present. Yes, Minnesota is the "land of 10,000 lakes," but not all of them will support a northern pike fishery. Lakes should have holes at least 15 to 18 feet deep to prevent winter kill by freezing out, especially those in the northern half of the state.

The Minnesota DNR has the authority to close up to 100 "experimental" lakes to spearing to protect muskie populations. The state fishing regulations list 38 Minnesota lakes as closed to spearing, including three of the state's largest: Mille Lacs (132,510 acres, 2nd largest lake contained wholly

Snow cleared from a northern Minnesota lake to prevent winter kill.

within the state), Cass (15,600 acres, 9th largest), and Minnetonka (14,528 acres, 10th largest). The anti-spearing lobby asks, "What harm can closing a few lakes do when there are so many?" However, these few lakes represent a disproportionately high percentage of the prime northern pike waters in the state, big lakes with good populations of food fish (e.g., tullibee and white-fish), and clear, deep water.

Recently slot limits on many lakes have served about the same purpose as closing lakes to spearing. For example, the slot limit for northern pike on Lake of the Woods is 30 inches or less and only one 40 inches or more. As more and more lakes have slot limits or are designated catch-and-release only, the opportunities for spearing will diminish.

Minnesota is currently talking about a statewide slot size for northerns of 26 inches or less, or more than 40 inches. This would greatly reduce, or even eliminate, darkhouse spearing opportunities in Minnesota.

The level of spearing activity in an area depends on (1) human popula-tion density, (2) availability of lakes, (3) clarity of lakes, and (4) ice, snow, and lake access conditions. Rural areas, although with fewer people in abso-lute numbers than urban areas, have a higher percentage of spearers. Coun-ties, like Otter Tail, with several hundred lakes, have more spearers than coun-ties with few lakes. Areas where runoff is high or where lakes are more eutrophic (nutrient rich, and thus less clear) have fewer spearers than areas where the lakes are clear. Although, the really clear lakes in northeast Minne-sota have far lower fish populations, due to a number of productivity factors.

There are plenty of rental darkhouses available in the popular winter fishing areas. However, there are no rental houses available on most of Minnesota's several thousand smaller lakes.

Catfish, Whitefish

Although it is legal to spear catfish in Minnesota, I have never run across anyone doing it or any references to it. The best catfish spearing would likely be on the Red River that forms the border between Minnesota and North Dakota, but spearing is not allowed in the Red. Of course, as with rough fish, catfish probably get speared incidental to spearing northerns.

Whitefish or tullibees, on the other hand, get some attention early in the spearing season since they are fall spawners. They are attracted into the hole with the usual northern decoys or with 2- and 3-inch long decoys. They are always on the go, so the spearer must be quick! There are no limits to the number of whitefish that can be speared. Most whitefish end up being smoked.

Rough Fish

Rough fish may also be speared in Minnesota darkhouses. Probably the most common would be eelpout, suckers, carp, bullheads, and gar, that sometimes swim through the hole at the wrong time!

Spearer Characteristics

I surveyed a sample of 1,922 Minnesotans who had purchased spearing licenses in 1986 to get a feel for who they were, how they fished, and what their attitudes were about spearing (Borge and Leitch 1988). Chapters 4 and 5 discuss the types and times various equipment is used. The following information was developed from 518 responses received.

Days fished. The average number of days fished during the 1986-87 season was 18 out of a possible 78 total. One person reported spearing 75 days that season. There are 22 weekend days and three holidays during Minnesota's spearing season. Winter's arrival, storms, snow cover, and work are each important factors in how often people go fishing.

Getting around is easy when there is little snow.

Sometimes good spearing holes are crowded, as here on Norway Lake in Otter Tail County, Minnesota.

Distance traveled. Thirty miles was the average distance traveled to spear, while some reported no travel (they lived adjacent to the lake) and those in central and west central Minnesota traveled only 8 to 11 miles. In other words, most spearing appears to be done by locals.

Age. Most spearers started spearfishing as youngsters with their fathers, uncles, or grandfathers. The average age of Minnesota spearfishermen is about 40 years; however, children and senior citizens also spear. But, since spearing is quite a bit more labor intensive than winter angling or summer fishing, there are far fewer very young or very old spearers.

Jobs. Almost half of all spearers are either craftspersons or technicians. The next largest group, about 17 percent, is farmers; however, only about 2 percent of Minnesota's population is farmers. Very few professionals or service industry employees participate in darkhouse spearing in Minnesota.

Expenditures. Minnesota's darkhouse spearers spent about $222 each during the 1986 season, or about $20 each day. On average, spearers spent the most on fishhouses ($45), followed by stoves and fuel ($24), chisels and ice augers ($22), transportation ($20), decoys ($20), spears ($10), and everything else ($81). (Note: these dollar figures could be inflated by about 40 percent to reflect 2001 prices.)

Spearing Impact Studies

Although the spearing controversy has gone on for years, few studies have been done to assess the impact spearing has on fish populations. This could be because DNR personnel believe, due to their experience and training, that darkhouse spearing has no appreciable effect on the resource. Or, it could also be that statistically valid studies are too expensive to conduct. However, MNDNR did studies in the mid-1950s, during the 1985-86 season, and recently.

Mid-1950s Study. The DNR did a study in the mid-1950s to compare the numbers of fish taken by spearers to those taken by anglers (Sonnenburg undated). Spearing accounted for 12 percent of the harvest in 36 lakes studied. Spearing accounted for 16 percent of fish catch by weight, since speared fish were larger than those caught by anglers. There was no difference in the numbers of fish harvested by the two groups.

The 1985-86 study was conducted on only three lakes near the Twin Cities — Buffalo, Howard, and Waverly Lakes (Treat 1987). It took an average of 8 to 12 hours longer to spear a northern than to catch one with hook and line. Winter anglers took more fish, but the average size was less.

The study was done in response to critics' claims that there was little current information on the impacts of spearing. No complaints or criticisms of spearing were voiced by the nearly 1800 ice fishermen, mostly anglers, interviewed on these three lakes. A mere 3 percent of the anglers interviewed were fishing for northerns.

A recent study. Pierce and Cook (2000) did a study of the changes in spearing effort and harvest over time and compared them with angling effort and harvest. They used several years' worth of creel survey data as well as harvest and catch rate data from the Minnesota DNR. They concluded

> ... summer and winter angling account for most of the northern pike harvest. Spearing accounted for 15% of the average yield of northern pike by number, but spearing is selective for the larger fish.
> .... Recreational angling, by comparison, removes an even greater proportion of all fish sizes in a population. Management designed to improve the size structure of northern pike populations will need to be directed at reducing harvest by all methods (page 239). Summer angling, when compared with spearing, harvests even more of the larger-sized northern pike (page 243).

Controversy

Darkhouse spearing in Minnesota is highly controversial and has been for some time (East 1959). Minnesota's DNR has pretty much stood by the sidelines, taking the position that northern pike populations fluctuate according to spawning success and that preserving spawning grounds is the critical factor in their numbers.

One of the arguments against darkhouse spearing is that too many illegal fish are speared. Illegally speared muskies get a lot of attention in Minnesota! When asked, Minnesota spearers reported that less than 10 percent of their spearing colleagues spear illegally. But, of course, all fishermen are liars!

Walleye were thought to be the fish most often speared illegally (77 percent of illegal fish speared), followed by muskie (11 percent), bass (11 percent), and all others (1 percent). Chapter 3 discussed both sides of the controversy in greater detail.

My First Minnesota Experience

Almost all of my darkhouse spearing experience has been in Minnesota, although I have speared in Alaska, Michigan, and South Dakota and witnessed spearing in Montana and Wisconsin. Much of this book either describes or is based on my Minnesota experiences.

My introduction to darkhouse fishing (spearing) was in about 1960 when I spent a few days in the darkhouse of the person to whom the first printing of this book was dedicated. I had been in a darkhouse a few times before with my dad, but only to be scared stiff when I saw what I thought was an alligator come into the hole.

On that first day on my own in the darkhouse, Jake had opened the hole, lit the stove, put the live decoy in the water, and left for town, leaving a twelve-year-old alone with a spear. I was excited to say the least, watching through a 2-foot by 2½-foot hole as a live 10-inch sucker swam around on a weighted line about 5 feet below the surface in about 8 feet of water so clear you could see a dime on the bottom.

It didn't take long for the first northern to shoot in, mouth wide open, and disappear with the sucker under the ice. Not knowing what to do, I just waited anxiously with spear in hand, heart pounding, for the fish to come back into view. Before long the sucker floated back, scarred by tooth marks, but no northern. This happened two more times before Jake returned. He then told me that all you need to do is gently pull on the line and you can usually pull the sucker, with the hungry northern attached, back into view. Not always, but most of the time this works. When the northern lets go, it more often than not comes right back in after the easy meal.

That introduction was the start of nearly 40 years of building darkhouses, chopping countless

The author's father with a Detroit Lakes hammerhandle in 1965. Spearers don't always take the big ones!

holes through the ice of countless lakes, and experiencing the heart-stopping entrance of many northerns. Those first three northerns on that late December day in 1960 were only 5 or 6 pounds, but with the distortion of the water and them racing in mouths wide open, they looked like alligators.

The chapter on "A Day in the Darkhouse" (Chapter 6) captures, as well as my writing can, the essence of my spearing experience in Minnesota.

Some Stories & Thoughts

Jiffy-Pop popcorn was always good when popped on top of my old kerosene stoves. I can't make popcorn any more with the propane heater. Becky prefers pretzels.

Cold morning. I once drove the snowmobile three miles to Twin Lake (near Amor, Minnesota), took the kerosene stove out and cleaned it out, cut the hole, fished, and rode the snowmobile home. I found out later it was 35 below zero that morning.

The tow job. A fellow fisherman asked me to tow his car off of Otter Tail Lake one day. I pulled it about 5 miles to shore, then up the bank, where I rolled back and broke the grill out!

Winterkill occasionally happens during severe winters when conditions cause oxygen levels to drop below minimums for fish survival. Once, while fishing on Bass Lake (Underwood, Minnesota) in late winter, I observed northerns swimming lethargically just under the ice, obviously from near-winterkill conditions. They were, however, feeding on small panfish, that were also schooled just beneath the ice.

Bad knot. Another time on Bass Lake I speared a decent-sized northern (about 8 pounds),

The author and son, Philip, with a 12-pound Pickerel Lake (Minnesota) northern in 1969.

only to see my spear drop 8 feet to the bottom without the rope! We even have that on video. The knot tying the rope to the end of the spear had come undone. It took about 15 minutes to rig something up to snag the eye in the end of the spear handle and pull it up with the fish on the business end. Fortunately, the fish was speared right behind the head, so it didn't swim off with the spear.

Shallow water. I usually like to fish in at least 8 feet of water or deeper, depending on water clarity. However, once during mid-winter I learned of some good fishing action on Lake Christina (Ashby, Minnesota). I followed the trail on the lake to where about 30 shelters were bunched up. I cut several test holes and each time found only about 3 feet of water. Finally I decided that must be as deep as anyone else was fishing so I cut the hole. It was odd staring into a hole with 18 inches of ice and 18 inches of water over a sandy bottom. It wasn't long before the perch started coming around and then the northerns. I speared my limit of three pretty quickly, after actually missing one in such shallow water. I only fished there that morning because the fish ran between 2 and 4 pounds. The lake winterkills often and there wouldn't be much chance of larger fish. In fact, the lake is famous for its canvasback duck populations and is managed for ducks rather than fish.

The **size limit** on Lake of the Woods (Minnesota) is under 30 inches and only one over 40 inches. The one and only time Becky and I speared there we saw lots of fish in the 26- to 34-inch range. We speared a couple 27 inchers. We saw a dandy come in and Becky wanted me to spear it — I didn't dare because it looked about 38 to 40 inches long. It hung around the hole for at least 30 seconds, offering me plenty chance to spear it.

My perceptions about northern behavior have been formed around watching them in the fishhouse. For example, my dad claims that dead sucker decoys, with their air sacs punctured so they sink to the bottom of the hole, attract fish. I guess they do, because he has speared a few with those same suckers in their stomachs! I had a hard time accepting the fact that northerns would eat a dead fish. In all the years I watched them in the fishhouse, I never saw one go after a lifeless decoy. But they do, and I have now even caught northerns on dead smelt during the summer.

Origin of the "northern pike." The Chippewa tell a story about a deity who was out to save some people but couldn't get across the river (Densmore 1979, p. 102):

The river was so mighty and terrible that even Winabojo could not cross it. As he stood on the shore he saw a little fish and said, "Little brother, can't you get me across this swift river?"

The fish said, "I am too small."

Winabojo said, "I will make you big." So he made the fish big and the fish took him across. In return for this he decorated the fish with spots and made his belly white. (This was a pickerel).

I hope spearing isn't outlawed in Minnesota during my lifetime so I can enjoy many more winters in the darkhouse and learn more about fish and fishing. I still get excited when the perch leave the hole and I'm always anxious to look into a freshly cut hole.

A proud spearer with an 18 pound 3 ounce northern from Clitherall Lake in 1989. "I bought a $53 spear two days before. I was in 16 feet of water. He came by on the shallow side going by very slowly out under the ice.: Ralph Woods, Vining, Minnesota.

■

For more information about darkhouse spearing opportunities in Minnesota, contact:

Minnesota Department of Natural Resources
500 Lafayette Road
St. Paul, MN 55155-4031
www.dnr.state.mn.us

Troy Schroeder with a 41-inch, 20-pound Lake of the Woods northern, winter 1999. Taken with a Duey's decoy.

A nice Lake of the Woods catch, showing Troy's spear with two extra tines.

Alaska

 Some type of subsistence darkhouse spearing may have been practiced in Alaska long before it was known in other parts of North America, especially if the practice came across an Aleutian land bridge. Sport darkhouse spearing was introduced shortly before Alaska became our 49th state, more than likely by spearers from Minnesota or Michigan. Spearing was legal before statehood, and continued to be legal after statehood was achieved in 1959.

While northerns are the main target of darkhouse spearers, whitefish and burbot may also be taken with spears during the winter in selected locations throughout Alaska. Alaska recently (1988) established a year-round season for using spears and bow and arrow for harvesting suckers and burbot (eelpout). They also established a year-round underwater spearing season for pike and whitefish, as long as the fisherman is completely submerged (Alaska Department of Fish and Game 1986).

In the past, eels (actually Arctic lampreys) were speared through the ice by Native Americans. Eels harvested through the Yukon River's thin November ice provide food for the native villages (Plein 1936).

Alaska annually issues about 150 darkhouse permits, for anglers as well as spearers. There are no other special licenses required, other than the regular angling license, and spearers must abide by angling limits (Kramer 1987).

Ice houses in interior Alaska, including darkhouses, must be registered with the Alaska Department of Fish and Game, which issues free permits. However, if ice houses are not left on the ice overnight, they do not need to be registered. Each house must have permit numbers displayed on the sides and the roof in distinguishable numbers not less than 12 inches in height. Roof numbers are required so they can be read from the air. Houses must be removed from the ice and the area around them cleaned up by April 30th (Doxey 1987).

Spears are made locally or "imported" from Minnesota, Michigan, or Wisconsin. Artificial decoys, too, are "imported" from the Midwest.

Northern Pike

Spearing for northern pike is legal from September 1 through April 30 in the entire Arctic-Yukon-Kuskokwim regulatory area, comprising most of Alaska. Some restrictions exist in very accessible areas near Fairbanks. However, northerns are found in almost all waters in Alaska. It wasn't until settling of former midwesterners in Alaska that northerns were thought of as more than dog food. The northern was made a game fish in 1957 and is now one of the most important game fish in interior Alaska (Alt 1984).

Northerns have become a nuisance fish in several Alaskan lakes. They compete too successfully with local trout populations.

Due to interior Alaska's extreme winters, the difficulties with transportation, and so many winter alternatives (like cutting wood), there may be no more than two dozen active darkhouse spearers in the state (Lambert 1988). Only a few good northern pike lakes are accessible by road; the rest are readily accessible only by air or snowmobile. By the time the ice is safe enough to land a light aircraft, it is so thick that cutting a spearing hole is a lot of work.

Registered guide Bill Lambert was the only guide who specialized in darkhouse spearing. He takes his spearfishing clients to prime pike lakes with a Super Cub on skis, a common form of transportation in Alaska. One of his clients has a mounted, 27-pound pike, nicknamed JAWS II, on display at the Fairbanks International Airport. The pike was speared in East Twin Lake in the Kantishna Flats.

Lambert's technique is to fly to his favorite pike lake, cut a hole through the ice with a chain saw, and erect a tent-like or pre-fab plywood darkhouse. He heats the light-free canvas and plywood darkhouse with a wood stove or kerosene moonlighter.

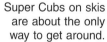

Super Cubs on skis are about the only way to get around.

Lambert's artificial decoys are either homemade or purchased from Wisconsin. The popular live sucker decoys in the lower 48 are not legal for use by darkhouse spearers in Alaska. In fact, no live fish can be used for bait in the state.

Darkhouse spearing in Alaska is not controversial, perhaps because of the low number of participants, the difficult conditions they typically fish under, and the frontier attitude of most Alaskans.

Whitefish

Some open water spearing, namely spearing whitefish in streams at night, is becoming more of a controversy in the state. This is primarily because of the difficulty in distinguishing whitefish from Arctic grayling. (I caught my first grayling in the Chena River in Fairbanks in June 2000!)

Whitefish may be speared from October 1 through May 31 in the Upper Copper-Upper Susitna River area and from September 1 through April 30 in the Tanana River drainage. Whitefish are speared at night using lights and, after the lakes freeze, from darkhouses. "The (whitefish) spear-fishery allows harvest of a fine food fish and provides excellent recreational opportunities for Alaska's sportsmen." (Chihuly 1983)

My First Alaska experience — 1989

Larry and I flew to Alaska in March to spear with Bill "Garfield" Lambert. After a restless night in a Fairbanks motel, we were up early to buy groceries (just a little more expensive in Fairbanks than in Minnesota), drive 40 miles to Nenana, and then fly another 75 miles to East Twin Lake.

The flight to East Twin in Bill's Super Cub was over the Minto Flats, a broad expanse of near featureless tundra. I watched intently for moose or wolves, but saw only tracks. Bill has one of the only two cabins on the 1200-acre lake, former home of JAWS II, the 27-pound northern on display in the Fairbanks airport.

We landed on a runway Bill had made earlier on the lake with one of two snowmobiles he kept at the cabin. There was almost two feet of snow on the ice, but a rain had created a thin sheet of ice on top of the snow, hazardous to the tail feathers of thin-skinned Super Cubs and also to moose.

The temperature was below zero, and a strong west wind blew while we unloaded a week's worth of groceries for three onto a sled behind the snowmobile. We made ourselves at home in Bill's cabin, which quickly warmed up from the fire in the woodstove. There wasn't much to do outside. The only wildlife around were a few red squirrels and Canada jays.

Lambert's "darkhouse",
F80, and snowmobile.

Five days of fishing were each about the same. We got up around 8 a.m., had breakfast, snowmobiled across East Twin to the darkhouse (the fish *always* bite better on the other side of the lake), opened the house and the hole, fished for about six hours, went back to the cabin to eat and tell stories before starting all over again the next morning.

Bill's house and equipment were atrocious! In order to get plywood to the lake he had to cut it into 2 by 4-foot pieces. The sides and roof of the 6 by 6-foot house were these pieces, with light coming through the cracks everywhere! We patched most of them with 100-mile-an-hour tape (duct tape).

Perhaps because Bill only fished when it was warm, or he didn't fish for long, or he wore plenty of clothes, there was no source of heat in the house. The second day out we brought along one of the kerosene heaters, a 'moonlighter,' from the cabin. It wasn't enough to keep ice from forming on the hole, or to keep us warm, but it sure helped, although it made the house smell like kerosene.

Bill's ice chisel was a lightweight, short-handled affair with a round cutting edge, but we got the hole open just the same. His two spears were the flimsy store-bought kind I complain about in Chapter 5. Both were lightweight and had short handles. OK, so the house wasn't light proof, and the chisel wasn't very good, and the spears were flimsy, but we were spearing in Alaska! I sent "Garfield" a Seeba spear (see Chapter 5) a few months after I got back to Minnesota. He bought another one, along with some decoys, while he was in Minnesota deer hunting that fall.

There were only a couple plastic Bear Creek decoys and some spoons to use. We did manage to get started fishing and within minutes there was a northern in the hole. In fact, almost every minute we fished for the next five

days there was at least one northern in the hole. More often than
not, there were two in the hole and
at least once there were four
northerns in view at one time.
Only rarely have I seen more than
one northern in the hole in the
lower-48.

JAWS II!

Not only were the northerns
plentiful, but they were hungry.
They hit the decoy and the line
so many times that the line finally
broke. Watching the decoy spiral
to the lake bottom is always a
little disheartening, but I had re-
covered many dropped items from the bottoms of Minnesota lakes. It just
takes patience and a steady hand. It wasn't until the third day, after the decoy
line broke, that I realized we were spearing in about 14 feet of extremely clear
water. That Bear Creek decoy probably still lays on the bottom of East Twin,
since I couldn't seem to snag it out.

Fourteen feet is a little deeper than I like for spearing. I was anxious all
week to try some other places on the lake. Thick ice (about 30 inches with a 2

The author with Alaskan
guide Bill Lambert on East
Twin Lake in March 1989.

foot snow cover), a poor chisel, and a heavy darkhouse kept me from moving around. Maybe next time.

It was easy to tease the northerns up to near the water's surface. Bill was fascinated the first time he watched me bring one nearly onto the fishhouse floor by teasing it with the decoy. An occasional fish had some distinguishing mark, such as a torn lip or a scratch on its back. Some of these were seen day after day, which makes me wonder how many of the hundreds of fish were actually some of the same fish just hanging around. The northerns ranged pretty much from 3 to 6 pounds. Since Alaska allows only one northern over 30 inches, we were careful not to spear the first 31-incher that came along. As it turns out, the trip trophy was only about 9 pounds. We didn't see any other fish species in East Twin Lake that week.

We had 10 northerns stacked up outside the cabin like cord wood (a small pile!). I sawed their heads off with a bucksaw, put them in a cooler, and shipped them home on the plane.

I returned to Alaska in October 1990 to spend a couple of months as a visiting professor at the University of Alaska-Fairbanks. As hard as I looked I could not find anyone who knew anything about darkhouse spearing, except what they could remember from living in Minnesota!

Alaska Again — 1994

There had been a 3-foot snowfall in early March, just days before we flew to Anchorage, rented a car, and drove 300 miles north to Nenana, home of the world-famous Nenana Ice Classic (www.optialaska.net\tripod). Within minutes after my phone call, Bill S. was checking out his ski-equipped Super Cub at the Nenana airport for our flight to E. Twin Lake. I had made the same flight four years earlier, but this was the first Alaskan fishing trip for my wife, Becky.

Bill S. and I arrived at the lake after a smooth 50-minute ride over the Alaskan landscape with Mt. McKinley visible on the horizon to the south. The InsTent was securely tied to the wing struts of Bill's SuperCub. I was met at one of the two cabins on the lake by Carol, Garfield's wife. Garfield (the other Bill) had taken Larry and I fishing at East Twin in 1989. Garfield had wanted to be there, but he was home in Fairbanks recovering from heart surgery.

Becky arrived two hours later. After carrying our gear the last 100 yards to the cabin and a short rest, we couldn't resist heading out onto the lake to cut a hole. There was about an hour or so of sunlight left. We began to cut a hole through the 30+-inch thick ice that afternoon. Surprisingly, the ice on E. Twin,

East Twin Lake

- 1 inch = 2350 feet
- Depth contours in 5 foot intervals
- Maximum depth 45 feet
- Altitude 692 feet

Prepared by Tom Simpson
1993
Alaska Dept. of Fish and Game
Division of Sport Fish

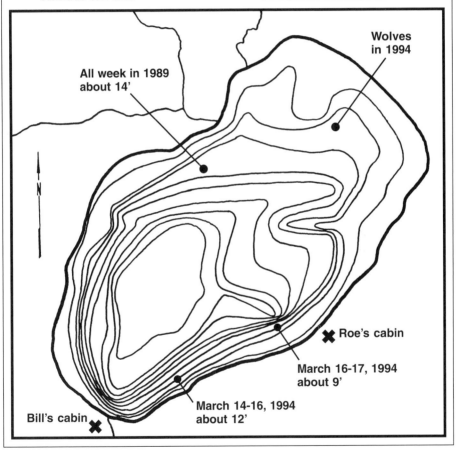

Wolves
in 1994

All week in 1989
about 14'

N

Roe's cabin

March 16-17, 1994
about 9'

Bill's cabin

March 14-16, 1994
about 12'

roughly 250 miles from the Arctic Circle, was no thicker than it had been on Oahe Reservoir in South Dakota the week before. Being a tradionalist, I still cut the hole the hard way, with a chisel, which was among the necessary darkhouse fishing equipment we brought along from Minnesota.

We were up early Monday to finish cutting the 2- by 4-foot hole we planned to peer into for the next five days. The foot or so of snow on the thick ice allowed little light to penetrate, so it was difficult seeing the bottom in 12 feet of water, even though the water was extremely clear. A few egg shells from breakfast scattered on the bottom provided the contrast necessary to see fish as they began to come in the hole.

We saw fish in the hole nearly constantly for the next 2½ days, attracted by one form or another of artificial decoy. Enough three pounders were speared for a couple meals. All the bigger fish the first three days came into the hole and left again without being speared — the spearers version of "catch and release."

By Wednesday afternoon I was ready to cut another hole. Becky fished while I cut a new hole about a ½ mile down the lake in 9 feet of water about 300 yards from shore. We moved the portable house and our gear to the new hole and fished a couple hours. It was much easier to see in the shallower water, especially after I shoveled off some of the snow around the darkhouse. We harvested six northerns about five pounds each from among the hundreds of fish we saw on Wednesday.

That night the timber (grey) wolves (*Canis lupus*) could be heard howling at the far end of the lake. When I went outside to listen, I noticed the magnificent northern lights dancing across most of the otherwise dark Alaskan sky. Although the thermometer read well below zero, the sights and sounds were spellbinding.

Thursday morning as we headed the long mile to the fishhouse we saw two moving dark spots at the other end of the lake coming our way. Before long we realized they were timber wolves. We walked east toward them and they trotted west for about 5 minutes, until they realized we were not prey. They turned tail and disappeared into the black spruce forest. I wished we had thought to lay down to see if they would have come closer, but Becky thought they came close enough as it was.

The overnight ice was skimmed from the fresh hole and we were fishing by 9 a.m. After only a few minutes the biggest northern I had ever seen swam slowly into view about 6 feet down with her eyes fixed on the red and white decoy. Seconds later a 44-inch, 28-pound Alaskan northern pike was flopping on the ice outside the darkhouse. This is what I had looked for in Minnesota for over 30 years and had come to Alaska for four years earlier, but had gone home without. Garfield had a 27-pound northern in the Fairbanks Airport taken from E. Twin Lake a few years ago, nicknamed "Jaws II." Now we had taken "Jaws III." An hour later another northern just as big swam into view, and again, we practiced "look at and let go." That trophy, as well as hundreds of others we had seen, most in the five- to ten-pound range, may still be swimming in East Twin Lake.

We speared four more, including one 10-pound northern for Becky, her biggest ever in five years of spearing. We had time to fish Friday morning, but what had happened on Thursday couldn't have been topped or even equaled, so we packed up the portable *InsTent* darkhouse as the sun hung low on the horizon and headed back to the warmth of the wood stove.

JAWS III, taken March 1994.

Becky and JAWS III. Ain't she a beauty?

44 inches of JAWS III next to my Seeba spear.

Friday we packed our gear, taking special care to pack "Jaws III" for her trip to an Anchorage taxidermist. The wind had blown hard two days earlier and the snow banks on East Twin were hard. Bill had to land on the protected side of the lake and taxi across the lake to pick us up, then taxi back to the protected side to take off. It was a beautiful flight back to Nenana, again with Mt. McKinley in view off to the south. There were moose and wolf tracks everywhere, a few moose, and one wolf-killed moose carcass in the spruce below.

Becky with the evening's meal from East Twin Lake.

I'll never forget the sights, sounds, smells, and adventure of that week in central Alaska in March. Jaws III is on my wall to remind me. Now that I have that wall hanger, only the eatin' size northerns need to be worried.

If I could spear in only one state ever again, it would have to be Alaska. I'm sure JAWS IV is somewhere in one of those lakes or rivers in northern Alaska.

■

For more information about darkhouse spearing opportunities in Alaska, call or write:

Alaska Department of Fish and Game
1300 College Road
Fairbanks, Alaska 99701
Phone: 907-456-8819
www.state.ak.us/local/akpages/FISH.CAME/adfghome

■

*I am no fisherman, and I hope
I never get lazy enough to take it up.*

Will Rogers

CHAPTER 9

Michigan

■

Ice fishing is the first sign of insanity.

Al McGuire
Marquette University basketball coach

 Obviously not everyone agrees with coach McGuire, since about 10 percent of Michigan's 1.5 million fishermen fish through the ice. As many as 10 percent of the ice fishermen, or about 15,000, are spearers (Fogle 1991), less than half the number in Minnesota. Spearers in Michigan, like their neighbors in Wisconsin, spear northern pike and lake sturgeon plus a number of other species (Michigan Department of Natural Resources 1989, Fogle 1983).

Unlike Minnesota, Michigan has both a longer spearing history and more modern day historians, many with a special interest in decoy carving (Fritz 1987, Kimballs 1986, 1987). Many of the commercial decoys found in bait stores in the Midwest come from Hastings, Michigan, home of Bear Creek decoys. The Kimballs' books on decoys are excellent references for the long and diverse history of decoy carving and carvers in Michigan. Nostalgia and the collecting bug have perhaps caught more people in Michigan than those who actually spear in winter!

Although Michigan's decoy culture gets a lot of attention, spearing hasn't received much (one of the reasons for this book). I did find a few published accounts in the popular press. Spearing in Michigan is discussed in a book by Zumbro (1978) in a chapter on "Unusual Icefishing Methods." He also includes some nice photos of a musky, northern, and sturgeon taken by spearers.

Michigan spearers are allowed to angle in the darkhouse while spearing. A spear is not considered a "fishing line" and it is legal to fish with two lines plus a spear per person. No special spearing license is necessary, just the usual fishing license. Michigan spearing regulations permit muskie spearing in certain lakes, something no other state does. Other species that are fair game to darkhouse spearers in Michigan include perch (but only in Lake St. Clair), sturgeon, catfish, whitefish, and a number of rough fish.

Fish houses are called ice shanties, shelters, and coops in Michigan. No house license is required; however, the owner's name and address must be shown on all sides of shanties in waterproof letters not less than two inches high. Only in Michigan-Wisconsin boundary waters is it illegal to lock shanty doors from the inside while fishing, and then only on the Wisconsin side. Shanties must be removed before the ice "becomes unsafe."

Northern Pike and Muskies

The season for northerns and muskies runs the months of January and February. By the way, muskellunge, or maskinonge, are Algonquian words meaning "great pike." Spearing is legal statewide except for designated trout lakes and other special management lakes (Michigan Department of Natural Resources 1989). Some areas are also closed to muskie spearing. There are minimum sizes of 20 inches for northerns and 30 inches for muskies, with longer minimums in some areas. Bag limits are five northerns and one muskie per day.

Decoys used include the many and varied artificials, suckers, perch, and shiners. While perch are a game fish, they may be used as decoys as long as they are caught legally.

Michigan has conducted one of very few somewhat scientific studies of the effects of spearing. For a number of reasons, in the early Sixties, the northerns in Fletcher Floodwater (Alpena and Montmorency counties in the northeast part of the lower peninsula) were not attaining the 20-inch minimum size. Special regulations in 1963 reduced the Fletcher minimum size to 14 inches, increased the daily limit to 10, and closed the area to spearing.

Northern fishing regulations were changed back to normal in 1967, except the spearing ban was continued. The DNR's study concluded that both harvest and size increased after the 4-year experiment (Beyerle 1971). While it is tempting to attribute some of the improvement to the spearing ban, it is more likely that reduced fish crowding and increased per fish food supplies were the prime reason for the change. The spearing ban merely traded winter harvest for summer harvest.

A couple of articles on northern spearing in Michigan should be available in your local libraries: "Great Lakes' Northerns" (Huggler 1987), which

Vernon Baggs, Sr. with a
36½# Muskie speared in
Round Lake in the 1960s.
Photo from Gary Miller's
fish decoy catalog No. 2.

mentions 'spear tossers' and "The Day the Pike Put the Move on Herman" (Rau 1977), a spearing article written about a series of live sucker decoys nicknamed 'Herman.'

Michigan northern spearing has even been written about in the *Washington Post* (Phillips 1986) in a nostalgic look at a transplanted Michiganite, living in Washington, D.C., who returns to spear in Munuscong Bay (just southeast of Sault St. Marie). He only gets one six-pounder on his fourth and last day. However, as usual in fishing, claimed, "Last week, you could have speared 50,..." The *Post* article captures the essence of a long day of waiting,

Eight hours later, a great northern pike rolled in like an angry bull, stopping inches from a decoy and fixing it with a deadly glare.

Lake Sturgeon

Sturgeon may be speared statewide on non-trout waters. Two fish may be taken per season as long as they are at least 50 inches long. The season runs the month of February. Black (about 10,000 acres), Burt (about 17,000 acres), and Mullet (about 17,000 acres) lakes in Cheboygan County, at the northern tip of the lower peninsula, are the most productive. The state record is a 193-pounder taken in 1974 in Mullet Lake (Michigan DNR Master Angler records).

Counts during the 1970s indicate that about 100 to 150 spearers went after sturgeon each year. No census was conducted during the 1980s, but an estimated 3 to 39 sturgeon are speared annually (Fogle 1991).

Sturgeon spearing on Black and Mullet Lakes was the best in more than 20 years in 1989. Only three were speared the entire 1988 season, but 16, from 55 to75 pounds, were taken on February 1, 1989 (Wolverton 1989). Water clarity and temperature are the keys to success; clarity to be able to see,

and temperature, to stimulate sturgeon movement. A sturgeon with a transmitter collar moved just 14 feet one February (Hacker 1989).

Sturgeon spearers are a patient lot, some spending 20 seasons without as much as a glimpse of a sturgeon. "Sturgeon spearing is as boring as watching grass grow or paint dry" (Richey 1990). I saw only about 75 shanties on Burt and Mullet Lakes in March 1991. Shanty rental is popular in this area, with prices from $30 to $50 per day (1991 prices) which includes all equipment and transportation on and off the lake.

Whitefish

Torch Lake, near Bellaire, is popular for whitefish spearers. They spear in 15-foot deep water, using spears 15 feet long (Wolverton 1989). To accommodate the long spear, they have holes in their shanty roofs!

Perch

Perch may only be speared in Lake St. Clair. Perch are attracted using the standard spearing decoys or special, minnow-sized decoys. Hank Walters, Sr., carved small, 3- and 4-inch minnow decoys (Baron 1988) and Ed Kellie also carved 2-inch "perchers" (Baron 1990).

My Michigan experience

Becky and I traveled to Michigan in February 1991 to conduct field studies for this book! We were able to spear one day in Portage Lake near Onekama in a shanty rented from a local motel for $20, plus $5 for a 16-ounce bottle of propane.

We left the motel in a near white-out blizzard, parked along Highway 22 near the public access, and walked 300 yards to the shanty. It took a little while to find the right shanty because of the extremely limited visibility; the wind was blowing about 30 to 40 mph directly into our faces. Snow kept blowing through cracks in the shanty and into the hole. Snow in the hole and ice forming on the water made it hard to see. The small heater was grossly inadequate for the dual task of keeping us warm and keeping the hole open.

The shanty was set up for perch angling, with a 1 by 4-foot hole. A small ax was all that was available for chopping out the ice; but we made do. The water was about seven feet deep and quite clear. We hung a green Lawrence Bethel decoy in the hole and fished for perch with wigglers (Mayfly nymphs). I felt guilty angling with a spear in the house!

Looking into the spearing hole at the "Travelers Motel."

An eatin'-sized northern from Portage Lake.

We saw plenty of perch (we didn't catch any), some nice-sized bass, and a huge carp (the first carp I've ever seen in a darkhouse). About 10 a.m. a 4-pound northern slid in, eyes fixed on the decoy. At first I didn't want to spear it, but I thought it might be the only one we saw, so... That was the extent of my spearing experience in Michigan.

carp

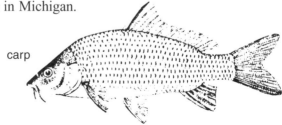

We visited with some other spearers and bait store operators and found that things are about the same as in Minnesota. There were far fewer houses than in Minnesota, however, very few in the U.P., and only a couple on lakes Michigan and Superior. It might be another case of too many other excellent outdoor opportunities in the winter.

Summary

Michigan offers a greater variety of species and methods of darkhouse spearing than any of the other five states. Nonresidents can spear in Michigan, and rental houses are available. Michigan also offers opportunities to pick up an antique decoy or have a meal of broasted chicken or pasties. However, I found there were far too many snowmobiles in Michigan!

■

For more information about darkhouse spearing opportunities in Michigan, call or write:

> Michigan Department of Natural Resources
> Box 30028
> Lansing, Michigan 48909
> Phone: 517-373-1270
> www.dnr.state.mi.us

Coops on Portage Lake, Michigan.

Montana

Darkhouse spearing was established as a legal method of fishing in Montana in 1969 (Needham 1986). It is allowed in all waters open to fishing in approximately the eastern two-thirds of the state. Northerns, walleye, sauger, burbot, and nongame fish are all fair game for darkhouse spearers (Montana Department of Fish, Wildlife & Parks 1989).

I am sure Minnesotans introduced darkhouse spearing to Montana. There are only a few hundred darkhouse spearers in the state, probably because of the many other outdoor opportunities and the vagaries of Montana's winters. As such, darkhouse spearing gets neither much promotion nor much criticism. Although angling through the ice is popular (Walcheck 1974).

Only a regular fishing license is required to spear in Montana, and nonresidents may spear in darkhouses. The season on lakes is year round, so

Darkhouses on Medicine Lake, 1990.

spearing can start as soon as the ice is safe and continue until ice-out.

Shelters (icehouses or shanties in Montana) according to Montana law include "...any form of hut or shelter constructed of canvas, cardboard, paper, plastic, poles or boards, sheet metal, pressed wood, or any other material, except those shelters or windbreaks constructed entirely of snow or ice." (Administrative rules of Montana 12.6.101).

Shelters must be identified with name, address, and/or phone number in legible letters at least two inches high, of contrasting color to the background, and plainly visible from the outside of the shelter at 100 feet. Shelter doors may not be latched from the inside. Shelters must be removed daily on some lakes and "before they are irretrievable via over-ice means" on others.

In the areas where spearing is not allowed, the maximum size hole that may be cut for ice fishing is 144 square inches, or one foot square, or a round hole with a 13.5-inch diameter.

Darkhouse spearing is constrained by law and by nature, by water clarity and ice conditions, to the eastern two-thirds of the state. Although Montana can have bitter cold winters, it can also have warm periods brought by the chinook winds.

Some of the lakes to spear are Medicine, Nelson, and Fort Peck Reservoir. There may be others too, depending on summer rainfall and winter ice conditions.

Notice the tie-downs on this Montana darkhouse to keep it from blowing away.

Medicine Lake

The first I heard of spearing in Montana was from a Minnesota DNR employee who made a trip each year to Medicine Lake in the northeastern corner of Montana. Medicine Lake is a 8,700-acre reservoir on a national wildlife refuge and is managed for waterfowl production. Because part of the area is designated wilderness, power augers are not allowed and vehicles cannot drive on the ice, making it somewhat inconvenient for spearing.

Usually no more than two dozen houses are on Medicine Lake at one time. The lake is shallow and has a carp problem, making visibility poor. They usually spear in only three to six feet of water, and some days cannot see the decoy.

Fish populations in this shallow prairie lake are highly influenced by droughts and low water, which can cause fish kills during both summer and winter. The five northern limit is easy to take on a good day, but they are generally under five pounds. Some as large as 15 pounds have been speared in the lake, however. Carp are also speared, but mainly to eradicate them.

Medicine Lake in northeast Montana.

Big Dry Arm, Ft. Peck Reservoir

Fort Peck Reservoir

Fort Peck Lake is one of several mainstream reservoirs on the Missouri River. The dam, completed in 1937, created a 220-foot deep lake, 134 miles long, with 1,520 miles of shoreline, and a surface area of almost 250,000 acres.

Much of the main reservoir does not freeze over in the winter. However, many bays get enough ice to support fishermen and fishhouses. Spearing is usually best in late winter when northerns begin to migrate to the bays in preparation for spawning.

Spearers on Fort Peck can expect to see some really large northerns, but they usually don't tell anyone when they spear them!

Montana Experience

I went to Montana on New Years Day 1990 with my portable house in the pickup. There were about 15 houses on Medicine Lake; most were near a couple of fishing access trails. After a bit of snooping around, I decided not to set up my house because the water was quite riled up.

Driving to Fort Peck about 125 miles to the southwest through the Fort Peck Indian Reservation was a pleasure. The wide open prairie broken occasionally by a coulee or butte is lovely when covered with a blanket of snow. It turned out that the drive was the most pleasant part of the trip to Fort Peck, since, when I got to the road atop the dam embankment, all I could see was open water!

I drove south along the Big Dry Arm to Rock Creek State Park. Here I visited with a Montana game warden who said there were a few spearers in one of the bays, but it was too early for the really good spearing. After cutting a few test holes in six inches of reservoir ice over six feet of crystal clear water, I packed up and headed home.

I did receive a couple invitations from Montana spearers after they read the first printing of this book. It sounded like they did pretty well as far as size goes, but sometimes the wait in between was a little long. And, like Oahe Reservoir in South Dakota, the water in Ft. Peck Reservoir isn't always clear enough to spear.

■

For more information about darkhouse spearing opportunities in Montana, contact:

Montana Department of Fish, Wildlife and Parks
1420 East Sixth Avenue
Helena, Montana 59620
Phone: 406-444-2950
www.fwp.state.mt.us

Guindon

GUINDON   MiNNeapOLiS Tribune

Herman Schmidt is just about fed up. He's going to do five or six more holes, and if he doesn't spear a fish with this dumb thing, he's going to return it to the hardware store.

South Dakota

Darkhouse spearing was introduced to South Dakota in the early 1960s, following establishment of a tremendous northern pike fishery in, then newly created, Lake Oahe, a 370,000-acre Missouri River reservoir. Darkhouse spearing was legalized in 1962 by the State Legislature.

A Minnesota spearer, who speared a 35-pound 8-ounce northern in Lake Sharpe in 1971, held the state's unrestricted record for 19 years. However, on February 24, 1990, Tom Cihak of Gregory, South Dakota, speared a northern in Lake Oahe weighing 36 pounds 1 ounce, setting a new record in the unrestricted class ("An Unrestricted Record" 1990).

Darkhouse spearing has not been controversial in South Dakota; however, underwater spearing has generated some controversy. Perhaps the reason darkhouse spearing has gone more-or-less unnoticed is because of the limited number of participants and the limited opportunity. Generally, the length of time that South Dakota fishing waters, especially the Missouri River reservoirs, have sufficient ice to support darkhouses is only a few weeks. This may be late in the winter when ice conditions make any activity on the ice somewhat risky.

There are only about 200 active spearers in the state, including a handful of nonresidents. When I asked a former Minnesotan, now living in Pierre, why he didn't spear given the excellent opportunities, he said because there were too many other winter activities, like predator calling!

All species of fish, except paddlefish and sturgeon, may be speared in South Dakota, the most liberal of any of the six states that allow darkhouse spearing. Daily and possession limits are the same as, and in combination with, hook-and-line limits. The winter spearing season runs from either freeze-up or December 1st, to early March. Winter spearing is legal only in Missouri River impounds, with some exceptions.

Fish may be taken with spears or legal spear gun. A legal spear gun is a muscle-loaded device propelling a spear attached to a lanyard no more than

20 feet long. Spears are either homemade, made by local blacksmiths, or bought from the same manufacturers who supply darkhouse spearing equipment in Minnesota and Michigan.

Ice houses must display the owner's name and address in letters at least two inches high. All shelters must be removed from the ice by March 5. No license is required for ice houses in South Dakota.

Darkhouse spearing is done in generally the same way as in Minnesota. Almost all Sough Dakota darkhouse spearers go after northern pike and spear other species incidental to fishing for northerns. The South Dakota Department of Game, Fish and Parks estimates the game fish harvest by darkhouse spearers to be insignificant in the State's annual total harvest.

Most spearing in South Dakota is done in the Missouri River reservoirs. The three large reservoirs are Lake Oahe, Lake Francis Case, and Lake Sharpe. Only under liberalized fishing conditions is it allowed in other waters of the state. As of early 2001, as many as 30 prairie lakes in northeast South Dakota were open to liberalized fishing.

Lake Oahe

One of the six Army Corps' Missouri River impoundments, Lake Oahe runs 231 miles from just south of Bismarck, North Dakota, to just north of Pierre, South Dakota. Oahe Dam was dedicated in 1962, the year spearing was legalized. The reservoir has 2,250 miles of shoreline and 370,000 surface acres.

Lake Oahe as 37 feet below normal in the winter of 1988-89, leaving many good northern bays high and dry.

Mobridge calls itself the "Pike Capital of the World." Twenty- and thirty-pound northerns are not uncommon in Lake Oahe. Test nettings in Lake Oahe have caught northerns almost equal to the angling world record size of 46 pounds. However, highly variable water levels and ice conditions make darkhouse spearing a gamble.

Lake Sharpe and Francis Case

Lakes Sharpe and Francis Case are merely wide spots in the Missouri. Lake Sharpe, a 64,000-acre impoundment, was created by Big Bend Dam near Fort Thompson, just north of I-90 about midway across the state. Francis Case, a 102,100-acre impoundment, was created by Ft. Randall Dam near Pickstown on the Nebraska border.

South Dakota – 1989

I traveled to the Mobridge area around New Years 1989. Oahe Reservoir was lower than it had been in years, due to a prolonged drought in the Midwest. Most of the usual spearing bays were high and dry. It was strange driving along the lake shore on what had been under 30 feet of water three years earlier.

I found a group of other fishermen that were angling walleyes, some were in houses, some were on the ice. Since walleyes are legal game, I set up next to them in about 8 feet of water.

The water was cloudy enough to need a few slices of potato on the bottom. Four hours later I had one 4-pound northern and had seen nothing else. But I had accomplished one of my objectives — to spear a northern in all states where it is legal.

Darkhouse spearfishing among the South Dakota prairie hills.

South Dakota – 1994

Becky and I left work at noon on a Friday in March 1994, got our gear loaded, and were on the road to Mobridge, South Dakota, by 2 in the afternoon. Along the way we saw deer herded along I-94 in North Dakota, as a result of heavy snowfalls that winter. Not until we neared the South Dakota border did we begin to see pheasants and grey partridge (also known as Hungarian partridge).

Mobridge is 300 miles from our home in Moorhead. We arrived in Mobridge at 7 pm, checked into the MoRest Motel, caught a few minutes of the Olympics on TV, and decided to call it a day.

Saturday morning we woke with anticipation as if it were opening day. We had breakfast and were ready to get going shortly before 8 a.m. The operator of the MoRest Motel is also a fishing guide, but he only guides in summer so he didn't know where the fish were in February! While Mobridge is the "pike capital of the world" in the summer months, only one bait shop is open in the winter. My conversation with the bait shop owner while I bought our family season nonresident fishing license (only $35) was less than encouraging. He said fishing had been slow all winter all along the reservoir's 300 miles.

Water levels were up this year, about 20 feet from the summer of 1992. This vastly changes the area covered by water and affects the availability of vegetation for cover.

Although I had some ideas where we might try fishing, I asked the bait shop owner for his suggestions. He said, "Few people actually fish northerns around here," suggesting there might be something wrong with fishing northerns. But he did offer a few places we might try, also noting that the ice was 30 inches thick and most locals had all but given up ice fishing for the season.

We drove to the Highway 12 bridge across the Grand River about 12 miles northwest of Mobridge. The highway and bridge create a narrow spot where the river's flow is concentrated and the current is increased. Oahe reservoir backs up the Grand River about 15 miles. Both up the river and down the river toward the Missouri mainstem are acres and acres of standing dead trees — trees that once lined the river banks. Some trees are mostly under water, while others are in only a few feet of water. Actually, we couldn't see any water, it was all frozen over.

We parked at the Grand River Recreation Area, one of 43 public facilities along Oahe, and questioned our sanity one last time before opening the pickup door to 15 to 25 mile per hour winds and temperature around 15 degrees F. I walked down the hill over the hard crusted snow banks to the river about 50 yards away while Becky added a few layers of clothing.

I tested the ice every few steps along the way with the ice chisel to be sure it was safe. My 15-pound chisel will go through 3 inches of ice with one jab. The ice seemed plenty safe. I went to the middle of the river about 30 yards out from the bridge and cut a test hole. The ice was about a foot thick. Dropping my high tech lead weight on a string depth finder through the hole, I discovered it was 12 feet deep, just a little too deep if the water is not perfectly clear.

I cut three more test holes, each one closer to shore, before finding a spot about 7 feet deep. By this time Becky had made her way down the bank without blowing away, just in time to head back to the pickup to get the gear while I started to cut a spearing hole.

This trip was also a shakedown cruise for a new portable darkhouse purchased for an upcoming icefishing trip to Alaska (March 1994). We wanted a darkhouse portable enough to check as baggage on commercial airlines, yet dark and sturdy enough to hold up under adverse conditions. As Becky began to set up the 5 x 5 1/5 foot InsTent darkhouse, we knew this would be a good test! The wind whipped the fabric around and nearly blew the shelter away.

With the shelter secured by two guylines and several large blocks of ice, we got the first look down the hole. The first look is one of the most anticipated moments in a darkhouse spearer's day. You never know what it is going to be like. Will the water be clear enough to see well? Will there be weeds on the bottom? Will there be trees, stones, an old tire, a pirate's treasure chest, or a boat motor on the bottom? Each hole has its own character.

The InsTent on the Grand River in South Dakota.

The bottom of this hole had a definite slope to it, from perhaps 5 feet on the right side to 8 feet on the left. The water clarity was a bit disappointing. When I tossed a few egg shells in the water, the current took them all under us and out of sight. Now we knew why the ice was only a foot thick here, as compared to the 30 inches we were told about.

Before long the water cleared up and we could see the bottom. Not too long later it clouded up again, so I pushed some egg shells down with my spear so they would land where we could see them.

With the heater going and the wind blowing, we watched down the hole for four hours without seeing anything except for the many different decoys we tried. I had hoped to see some big northerns that had begun their move up the tributaries in anticipation of spring and spawning. Northerns are the first to spawn in the spring, often before the ice is off the lake. The days were getting longer and there had even been a few warm days causing snowmelt and runoff. I guess we were just a few weeks early. We decided to try somewhere else nearer the mainstem of the Missouri River.

There were very few fishhouses on the ice, but we did see a few on the way back to Mobridge. We checked out a couple places along the Grand River, but were hesitant to drive on the ice since we thought it was only a foot thick. A foot is enough to support a vehicle, but I was unfamiliar with the area and didn't want to take any chances. Also, since all the houses we saw were quite large, they appeared to be angling houses.

The ice can get thick on Lake Oahe!

We headed to the Indian Creek Army Corps recreation access about three miles south of Mobridge, which seemed like a good place to ambush a northern! There were two anglers watching some tip-ups about 200 yards away from where we drove on the ice. We cut a test hole to find 30 inches of ice and 30 feet of water. The second hole was 20 feet of water, but the third was just right, about 9 feet. It took nearly an hour to get the hole cut and get set up using just a chisel and an ice saw.

The wind was still blowing as we stepped into the house to experience another first look down a new hole! The water was crystal clear, making it easy to see there was nothing on the bottom except a few rocks. Three hours watching the lake bottom went by slowly. All we saw was a 2" minnow of some kind that kicked up some silt on the bottom. Two other groups of anglers drove by, setting up near the two already sitting on the ice.

When we packed up at about 6 o'clock, only two anglers were left — sitting in their vehicle with the motor running to keep warm. A few weeks earlier it would have been dark at this time, but there was almost another hour of light left. Time zones change at the Missouri River, so it was an hour earlier on the west bank.

We had a nice dinner at The Wheel Restaurant overlooking Lake Oahe and the sunset. After watching some more Olympics on TV, we discussed plans for Sunday. Our enthusiasm had been dampened by a long day without seeing anything over 2". We decided to try one more place in the morning.

Sunday morning was bright, calm, but cold — a relief from the high winds and wind chills of the day before. A quick stop for "breakfast" goodies from a grocery store and we were on our way. We headed north along the east side of Lake Oahe, having our traveling breakfast and looking for Rongo Bay, an Army Corps access point. We stopped to watch a golden eagle sitting on a post right next to the road. It flew about the time we came to a full stop, but it flew along the road just yards above the ground for a half mile; what a beautiful sight. In the 20 miles to the access point we also saw several bunches of sharptail grouse, some grey partridge, and a dozen or so deer. Highway 1804 runs atop the hills and ridges between rolling rangeland and the Missouri breaks. If nothing else happened that day, it had already been worth getting up for.

The gravel road to Rongo Bay had not been plowed, and even though we had a 4-wheel drive pickup, we dared not try going through the deep snowdrifts. A few miles farther, at the West Pollock access we saw vehicle tracks on the ice and a few fish houses scattered around the mile-wide entrance to 4-mile long Pollock Bay.

We drove to near an angling house, turned toward shore, about 150 yards away, and begin cutting test holes. After the fourth test hole through 30+ inches of ice with aching muscles from the day before, we went midway between holes three and four. It looked like a perfect area for northerns, the shore was gently sloping, there was brush lining the bank, and it appeared to be a broad area of likely northern habitat.

After a tiring hour of chopping and sawing, we stepped inside to our third first look into a new hole in two days. Perfect! It was just over 10 feet deep and clear as a crystal. The lack of weeds or other cover was disappointing, but only 18 months earlier this area had been high and dry.

With renewed anticipation we watched and waited, tried many different decoys, tried some winter angling spoons and jigs, and munched on what was left of our breakfast goodies. Since the InsTent has small windows on two sides, we occasionally looked out to see activity a few miles away near some angling houses, and a few vehicles drove past us on the way to their hot spots.

About the time we were noting how nice it was without the wind blowing the shelter's fabric walls around, a snowmobile approached. It circled us and stopped. The usual "how ya doin" came at our door. Glad to have someone to talk to, we invited him in. He and his buddies had spent the night fishing for walleyes in a large fishhouse with bunks. They hadn't caught a thing. We had a nice conversation, finding out that we had some mutual friends back home, 300 miles away. Amazed at how he could see so well into the water, the snowmobiler left saying he would be back next year with a darkhouse.

We packed it up at 2 o'clock and headed for home, having not seen one fish in about 10 hours of watching down the hole. On our way out two days earlier, we were concerned about South Dakota's limit of one northern over 36" per day and if we would have room in the cooler for northerns and walleyes! The cooler was still empty but the fishing was good. We had looked through three fresh holes in the ice in three very different parts of Lake Oahe, eaten well in local restaurants, seen a golden eagle and other wildlife, visited with others about fishing, gotten some exercise, and figured out what needed to be done to the shelter before Alaska. We chopped through at least 24 feet of ice for test holes and removed at least 36 cubic feet of ice for spearing holes — but the fishing was good!

Our 2½ days fishing cost us $66 for two nights lodging, about $50 for food, about $30 for gas, and $35 for a family nonresident season license. It was well worth it, even though the cooler came home empty.

"If at first you don't succeed..."

I've made at least two more trips back to Lake Oahe to spear in winter. On one trip, the water was so cloudy that I went home the day I got there. On another trip,- we saw one small northern and ended up angling walleyes in 40 feet of water.

■

For more information about darkhouse spearing opportunities in
South Dakota, contact:

      South Dakota Game, Fish and Parks Department
      523 East Capitol
      Pierre, South Dakota 57501
      Phone: 605-773-3485
      www.state.sd.us/gfp

Looking for a spot on Lake Oahe.

North Dakota

After several failed attempts in the 1990s to legalize darkhouse spearing in North Dakota, *House Bill 1356* became law in April 2001 when it was signed by Governor Hoeven. HB 1356 requires the governor to provide by proclamation for spearfishing through the ice from dark houses, allowing nonresidents to spearfish from darkhouses in North Dakota only if their state of residency allows North Dakotans to spearfish from darkhouses. Since Minnesota prohibits nonresidents from darkhouse spearfishing, Minnesota residents will not be allowed to spearfish in North Dakota.

Specific provisions of the law — such as what species will be legal to spear and when the winter spearfishing season will be — will need to be worked out by the Department of Game and Fish. North Dakota law currently prohibits fishing holes in the ice from exceeding 12 inches in diameter or 12 inches square — this will need to be changed to facilitate the larger holes needed for winter spearfishing.

Several abnormally wet years leading up to 2001 have created tremendous northern pike and yellow perch fisheries in many areas where fish could not survive 10 years earlier. Of course, drier conditions could take this resource away just as fast.

Typically North Dakota has about 400 fishable lakes. The three lakes with the most promise for winter spearfishing are Lake Sakakawea, a 500,000-acre reservoir on the Missouri River; the upper end of Lake Oahe, another Missouri River reservoir; and Devils Lake, a closed-basin lake with nearly 111,000 surface acres in 2001.

The Director of the North Dakota Game and Fish Department, Dean C. Hildebrand, personally championed the darkhouse spearing bill through the Legislature.

I think there is a genuine interest in a new sport for our North Dakota winters: Darkhouse spear fishing. It could be attractive for northern pike on certain lakes that have water clear enough to allow for this sport. It will spark a new effort in equipment sales. Seminars and educational material will be provided on how to use the equipment successfully and safely. People will travel great distances to experience this unique opportunity. It will provide for another recreational opportunity for both residents and nonresidents in our great North Dakota outdoors. There is great potential for this fishery. (Quoted in an e-mail from Director Hildebrand on April 11, 2001.)

■

For more information about darkhouse spearing opportunities in North Dakota, contact:

North Dakota Game and Fish Department
100 North Bismarck Expressway
Bismarck, North Dakota 58501-5095
Phone: 701-328-6300
www.discovernd.com/gnf/

Wisconsin

 Northern pike and lake sturgeon are both sought after by darkhouse spearers in Wisconsin. Due to the limited opportunity for, and participation in northern spearing, I will only provide a brief sketch. However, sturgeon spearing gets much more attention in the state and it will in this chapter also. Finally, for the sake of completion, I feel compelled to mention the open-water spearing controversy that exists in Wisconsin.

Darkhouse spearfishing may have originated in Wisconsin. The Kimballs (1988) present a nice history of winter spearfishing by the Ojibway people of Lac du Flambeau. Although they have a propensity for slight exaggeration ("the hole must be perfect or the whole technique may not work" p. 21), the Kimball's book is an excellent source of information and photographs. Winter spearfishing continues on some reservations, with a few dozen participants.

Some Native Americans also spear muskie through the ice from darkhouses or, the more traditional, wigwam (Meyer 1991, p. 60).

> *Lac Courte Oreille tribal members...spear muskellunge and a few walleye and northern pike through the ice on the Chippewa Flowage and other reservation border lakes from darkhouses (shacks covered with felt). Some spearers use hand-carved wooden decoys to attract fish;..others "jig" for trout...and use them as bait...Lac du Flambeau fishermen spear muskellunge through the ice from 3 to 4 foot high "wigwams"...of branches and covered with cloth material. A blanket is placed on the snow.., and the spearer lies on it with his head and shoulders inside the wigwam...During the winter of 1986-87,....the total number of spearers was between 62 and 124. Total winter harvest...was between 250 and 350 muskellunge.*

Recreational, through-the-ice, spearing was in Wisconsin as early as 1873 (Jacobstaff 1873):

We built a small movable house on the ice, in which we rigged up a small stove, had cushioned seats, and other things comfortable, and the way we did slaughter those muscalonge [sic] was a sin and a shame. Thus we were the first, I believe, to introduce on Beaver Lake that style [darkhouse spearing] of fishing.

This account of 19th century spearing in Wisconsin led to others which led to "... destruction... so great that the citizens had to interfere and put an end to the practice entirely." The state prohibited methods other than hook-and-line for taking game fish in 1878.

Northern Pike

Northern spearing is limited to Lake Superior and the Menominee and Brule Rivers (and their impoundments) that border Michigan. Spearing is not permitted in other waters of the state and ice fishing holes can be no more than 12 inches across (Wisconsin Department of Natural Resources 1991, 1991a).

Due to the limited areas where spearing is allowed and to the year-to-year uncertainties about ice conditions in the rivers and lake Superior, there are not very many darkhouse spearers who pursue northerns in Wisconsin, perhaps as few as 100. Those that do, do it just like spearers in Michigan and Minnesota.

The spearing season is January and February with a daily creel limit of five. No special license is necessary. Doors of fishing shelters must be readily openable from the outside while occupied. The shelter owner's name, in letters at least one inch square, must be permanently attached to the outside.

Sturgeon

Sturgeon spearing gets much more publicity in Wisconsin than does northern spearing. The Menominee Indians of Wisconsin speared sturgeon as early as 1837 (Baumann and Jaeger 1983).

Sturgeon spearing is permitted every year in Lake Winnebago (137,000 acres) and every five years in Buttes des Morts (1300 acres), Poygan (14,100 acres), and Winneconne (4,500 acres) lakes and connecting waters. Winnegabo, Indian for "dirty, stinky, or ill-smelling water," is by far the largest of these lakes, being 10 miles wide and 35 miles long with a maximum depth of 21 feet and an average depth of 18 feet.

A special sturgeon spearing license and tag are required. These were $7.00 in 1991. As many as 10,000 people will purchase spearing tags in a good year. Sturgeon spearers must be at least 14 years old. Only one sturgeon may be taken per year, and it must be registered with the DNR.

The sturgeon spearing season starts the second Saturday in February and ends March 1 in Lake Winnebago. It only lasts two days in the other areas! A license must be purchased within the first two days of the season. I visited Lake Winnebago in February 1991, one day after the last day to buy a sturgeon license! However, given the success of sturgeon spearing, I was probably lucky to have saved the $7!

Sturgeon must be at least 45 inches long to be legal to spear. There are no restrictions on hole sizes for sturgeon spearing.

Due to the size of sturgeon, spears are much larger than the usual darkhouse spear. They have six- to ten-foot handles and are often weighted to help penetrate the sturgeon in 12 to 14 feet of water. Most sturgeon spears have detachable heads attached to 30 to 50 feet of rope (Dornbrook 1948).

Sturgeon use their rubbery vacuum cleaner snout to feed on clams, crayfish, and some aquatic plants (Griffin 1985). However, a variety of decoys is used to attract the curious sturgeons' attention and to help judge their size. Tin cans, oranges, lemons, ear corn, artificial fish, even model airplanes are used to lure sturgeon into range. Decoys also provide a reference point for judging a sturgeon's size and its location.

Sturgeon spearing shanties are larger than those used to spear northerns, since the spearing hole might be 4 by 6 feet. This not only permits more area to be seen, but allows room to land a 5- or 6-foot fish weighing up to or over 100 pounds. Over 3400 sturgeon spearing shanties have been counted on Lake Winnebago at one time.

Rental shanties are available from several outfits in the Fond du Lac area (Fond du lac Convention & Visitors Bureau). Rental fees are from $30 to

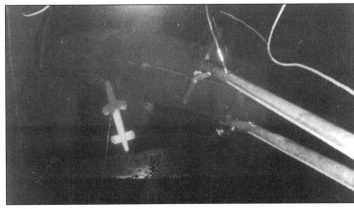

Is this sturgeon over 45 inches?

Here it is out of the hole, 99 pounds! Speared in Lake Winnebago by Larry Margelofsky, of Vandyne, Wisconsin.

$45 per day, including the spear, decoy, and heat. Entrepreneurs are also available to cut the spearing hole. The cost was $8 for a 4x6 foot hole in 1991, which is quite reasonable since the ice is usually at its thickest in March.

The success of sturgeon spearing varies according to water clarity and fish movement. Good snow cover on the ice reduces algal blooms and improves water clarity (Baumann and Jaeger 1983). Harvests as high as 2,220 have been recorded in 1955 and as low as 30 in 1983. Harvest averaged 651 fish during the 36-year period from 1955 to 1990. The 1990 annual harvest was almost 3000 sturgeon.

The state spearing record is a 180-pounder taken by Elwood Schroeder in 1953 (Bauer 1958). A 160-pounder was taken in 1986. Sturgeon that big may be well over 50 years old. A 20 year old sturgeon will be about 53 inches long and weigh 35 pounds; at 30 years it will be 59 inches and 53 pounds; and at 40 years it will be 69 inches and 85 pounds. Females do not mature until 24 to 26 years old (Baumann and Jaeger 1983). These are all good reasons for closely monitoring and managing sturgeon harvests.

Spearfishing by Native Americans

A type of spearing in Wisconsin that has been highly controversial is open water, nighttime spearfishing by Native Americans, mainly for walleyes (a few also spear muskies and bass), during the spring spawning run (Krueger 1985, Krueger 1985a, Gardner 1987). Spring spearing is a part of Native American culture. They insist it is cultural and economic, but most sport fishermen do not condone it. Violent confrontations have occurred over the past several years between Indians and those opposed to their being able to spear during spring spawning runs. However, some of the heat over this issue may now be subsiding.

Almost all of the fish harvested are walleyes. The harvest is closely monitored by the Wisconsin Department of Natural Resources, who doesn't think the annual harvest of 3 to 5 percent of adult walleye by fewer than 400 spearers is detrimental to the resource (Busiahn 1990). A recent Congressional inquiry, responding to the growing controversy, concluded that fish populations are not being over exploited in most cases (Meyer 1991). However, on some waters the harvest by anglers is reduced by lowering creel limits in order to prevent over harvest.

Culture, tradition, and the need for food are arguments used by Native Americans in support of their open-water spearing. Yet, the Wisconsin Chippewa only began spearing spawning walleyes in 1983. But, how traditional are aluminum boats, outboard motors, and halogen spotlights?

On a related issue, an Alaskan court recently ruled in favor of native claims that it was part of their culture to hunt from snowmobiles, since they had done so for 20 or 30 years. Darkhouse spearing has been part of the culture of some areas of the Midwest for several generations — shouldn't that, too, also qualify as a reasonable part of culture, worthy of preservation?

The only purpose for mentioning Native American spearing here is to note that there is a difference between it and darkhouse spearing. (Some useful references are Meyer 1991, Busiahn et al. 1989, Thannum 1990, and GLIFWC undated). Native American spear fishing is being treated as a treaty rights issue, a racist issue, and a question of sport. The later is related to the darkhouse spearing controversy discussed in Chapter 3.

■

For more information about darkhouse spearing opportunities in Wisconsin, contact:
Wisconsin Department of Natural Resources
Box 7921
Madison, Wisconsin 53707
Phone: 608-267-6897
www.dnr.state.wi.us

Part IV
Precautions and Predictions

CHAPTER 14

Ice Fishing Safety

People are hurt or die each winter while ice fishing; some drown, others have heart attacks or are asphyxiated, and others get hurt. The Minnesota DNR has recently been running a radio and TV ad campaign that warns people of the dangers of driving on the ice. (I wonder why they don't warn them about downhill skiing? Or broom ball?) People think I'm nuts for even wanting to be on the ice. Nonetheless, a few precautions and some common sense can prevent needless injury.

Drownings

There were 109 ice-related drownings in Minnesota from 1976 to 1990, or about seven each year. In the time between printings of this book, from 1991 to 2000, there were 58 ice-related drownings. Around half of these had nothing to do with fishing, leaving an upper estimate of three ice fishing related drownings in Minnesota per year. Even one drowning is too many, but given the number of participants and the number of hours fished, ice fishing is relatively safe.

Cars have been falling through the ice on Minnesota's lakes for several decades.

Thin ice sign near open water on Leech Lake.

Annual Ice-Related Drownings in the Six Spearing States*

State	Ice-Related Drownings	
	Total	Fishing
Alaska	not available	
Michigan	8	3
Minnesota	7	3
Montana	none known to be fishing related	
South Dakota	none known to be fishing related	
Wisconsin	not available	

*The numbers represent averages over a number of years.

Other types of injury and fatalities while ice fishing include asphyxiation, heart attack, hypothermia, and accidental injury, such as getting caught in the power auger. There are no available statistics on the numbers of these types of problems related to ice fishing.

Asphyxiation and Carbon Monoxide Poisoning

Asphyxiation, the result of a shortage of oxygen, results when the darkhouse is too airtight and the heater uses up oxygen. Carbon monoxide, a colorless, odorless and very toxic gas, poisoning results from incomplete combustion of carbon. Asphyxiation and carbon monoxide poisoning are probably the cause of a couple darkhouse related deaths each year across all six states and, like drownings, could be avoided.

My cousin and his son-in-law left for home after several hours in the fishhouse on Wall Lake (Fergus Falls, Minnesota). Less than ten minutes later, as they drove onto the highway, my cousin died of carbon monoxide poisoning. Fishhouses need not be this dangerous.

Heart Attacks

Heart attacks may be the cause of the most ice fishing related deaths. Spearing is physically arduous, especially when it is time to move the darkhouse and cut a hole through thick ice. Common sense should be the rule — just take it easy or get someone else to help out.

Accidents

There are any number of ways that an accident can happen while ice fishing. People can slip and fall on the ice. Cleats or creepers are available to help walk on slippery ice. People can strain something lifting, pulling, or pushing the darkhouse. Clothing can get caught up in power augers. Chain saws can cause serious injuries. People can get burned by the stove, frostbitten from the cold, or snowblind from the sun. Common sense and a few precautions will avert all but a few of these.

When is Ice Safe?

When it's in your lemonade. But seriously, the ice on the lake is never completely safe! It can be thick enough to walk on and to drive on if some caution is used. The ice should be even, well-formed blue ice (Brazier 1985). The rule-of-thumb is that 2 to 4 inches will support one person, 5 inches will support a snowmobile or ATV, and 8 to 12 inches will support an automobile (Elverum 1979). However, ice is not always the same, some 1-inch ice will support a person, while other 12-inch ice will not.

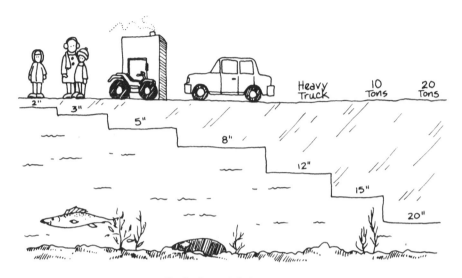

Safe ice thickness.

Several examples of what has been done on frozen lakes illustrate the strength of ice. The train used to cross the Missouri River between Bismarck and Mandan, North Dakota, only when the ice became thick enough to lay tracks across. Many developments in northern areas of Siberia and Canada are only accessible in winter when roadways are made across a landscape of lakes. Road graders and snowplows are used to plow roads to fishhouse villages on many of Minnesota's lakes. Our 10' by 12' angling house got desperately blocked in deep snow on Otter Tail Lake as the end of 1965-66 season approached. My dad drove an International HD-5 crawler four miles across the lake to retrieve it. The ice cracked and popped, but we made it.

There are also many stories of the ice giving way underneath the weight of vehicles. For example, a housemover once discovered that the ice of Lake Superior was not strong enough to hold his truck and the house he was moving to an island in the lake.

The strength of ice depends on thickness, water depth, size of lake, water chemistry, load distribution, and local climatic factors (Elverum 1979). Water depth plays an unusual role in ice strength. Weight moving on the ice causes waves in the ice. At "critical speeds," that depend on water depth, the ice may crack (Little 1975, Elverum 1979). Driving faster or slower than these critical speeds is safer; slower may be both safer and wiser.

Water depth	Critical velocity
4 feet	9 mph
6 feet	11 mph
8 feet	12 mph
10 feet	14 mph
15 feet	17 mph
20 feet	19 mph
30 feet	22 mph

In other words, driving 14 mph over 10 feet of water will cause ice waves and may lead to cracks and falling through. It is safer to drive 12 mph over 10 feet of water, but not over 8 feet of water! It seems like these critical velocities are an interesting phenomenon, but how can you keep that close track of water depth?

Ice doesn't freeze uniformly all across the lake. Inlets, springs, fish schooling, snow cover, and pressure ridges can each affect how thick and how strong the ice is at a point. Most people whose vehicles fall through the ice were very familiar with the lake, but the wrong combination of events led to bad ice conditions. In one case in central Minnesota, late fall rains resulted in much higher and warmer than usual runoff, which, in turn, caused weak spots in the ice and many vehicles went through.

Did you ever wonder why ice floats? First and foremost, so we can go icefishing. Actually, ice floats because it is lighter than water. If ice didn't float, there might not be any fish life in most northern waters.

Water is heaviest (most dense) at 39.2 degrees Fahrenheit (about 4 degrees Celsius). In other words, a gallon of water either warmer or colder than 39.2 degrees F will be lighter than a gallon at 39.2 degrees F. (A gallon at 39.2 degrees F weighs 8.33 pounds, while at 32 degrees it weighs 8.32 pounds.) This means that ice is lighter than the warmer, unfrozen lake water and, thus, floats on top. If ice were more dense (heavier) than water, it would form on the lake bottom. The deepest lakes in "spearing country" would be ice cubes year around.

This physical property of water is also what causes many lakes to "turnover" in the spring and fall. Actually, the cold water is on top in the winter and on the bottom in summer because of what I explained above.

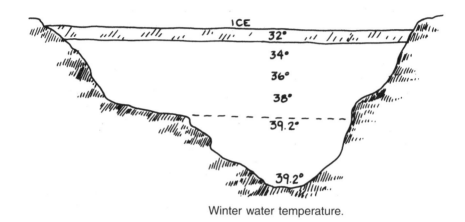

Winter water temperature.

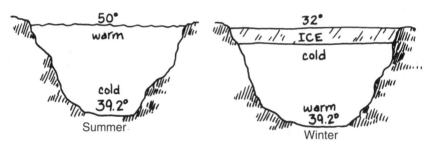

Water temperature "turnover" from summer to winter.

Ice fishermen fall through the ice when walking, when riding snowmobiles or ATVs, and when driving. Airplanes occasionally go through the ice as well.

Walking on the ice is the safest way of getting around. You can see, hear, and feel the ice, as well as check with a chisel as you go.

I fell through a 2-foot wide crack in the ice that had just frozen over and was blown over with snow. It was a breathtaking experience and walking the mile to shore in below zero temps and strong wind was no picnic, but I was in no real danger. Another time I walked across a small lake in the middle of winter, thinking the ice was 30 inches thick all over. I would test it with my chisel once every 100 feet or so. Right in the middle of the lake the chisel went through like there was no ice; it wasn't even an inch thick.

Times when it isn't that easy to get out after falling through the ice can be dangerous, as humans will last about 20 to 30 minutes in the near freezing water (Thomas 1989). Always carry a pair of ice picks on a string around your neck to help pull yourself from the water should you fall through thin ice.

Riding a snowmobile or ATV on the ice is more dangerous than walking because you're both going faster and you can't hear as well. It's still probably less dangerous than a car or pickup because you won't be trapped inside if it falls through. The advent of snowmobiles and ATVs may have reduced the percentage of fishing related-incidents, but might have increased the overall number of ice-related drownings.

Darkhouses, too, sometimes fall through the ice. This happens before the ice is thick enough, after heavy rain or snow, and as the ice melts in the spring. Small, portable houses can be pulled on the lake when there is only enough ice for one person to walk on. Larger, more elaborate fishhouses can't be used until the ice reaches 8 or 10 inches thick.

My 6' by 6' darkhouse on wheels fell through 4 or 5 inches of what I though was good ice on Elbow Lake (also known as Bass Lake, NW of Battle Lake, Minnesota). There were several other houses on the lake so I thought it was safe. I cut the hole, pushed the house over the hole, and water started coming up on the ice. In about 30 seconds one corner of the house dropped through the ice — door side down! I was lucky to not be in the house as it went down. A week later, Dad and I chopped and jacked it out of the ice.

Darkhouse #3, I should have waited!

There was a piece of ice, 5 inches thick, diagonally across the house where the water line had been. That was the last season I used that house.

Vehicles falling through the ice usually make news wherever it happens. Some winters there are many of them that go through and other winters very few. The weight of a parked car on 12 inches of ice can depress the ice about 1 inch. Imagine what several cars parked close together can do!

While some people suggest following a well traveled trail across the ice, others say to avoid them because constant traffic weakens the ice. I was driving on a highly traveled trail on about 30 inches of ice over a foot of water when the front of my pickup dropped into a 2-foot wide crack. I could see water on the trail ahead, but had no idea the crack was so wide. We stopped instantly, water splashed everywhere, the minnow pail tipped over, and the front of the pickup was wrecked. Fortunately, no one was hurt. The tow truck driver would not drive on the ice, so we had to winch the pickup up the bank, between the trees.

There are a couple ways to recover a vehicle that has fallen through the ice. Most common is waiting for the ice to get thicker, finding a tow truck driver willing to go on the ice, cutting a large hole, and winching the vehicle up. The deeper the water, the more complicated this gets.

Another way is to wait for spring, then float the vehicle to the surface by inflating inner tubes inside the vehicle, and float it to shore where it can be towed away. One unlucky soul marked his sunken vehicle with a float, only to have the ice tear the float loose — he never found the vehicle again. So many vehicles were going through the ice on Devils Lake, North Dakota, that an enterprising person built a large tripod device for hoisting them to the surface. In any case, it can cost thousands of dollars to recover a sunken vehicle. Some insurance companies will cover these costs. The greatest cost is the possibility of drowning and the embarrassment of losing your vehicle.

As a precaution, drive slowly with a door ajar and ready to be opened as an emergency exit. Vehicles usually float for a few seconds, perhaps up to a minute, before sinking. If your vehicle breaks through, stay calm. It may float or get hung up on the ice long enough for you to get to safety; if not, wait for it to hit bottom and find a way out while it is filling with water.

A situation unique to big waters and rivers is having large pieces of ice break away and float into open water. This happens often in the Great Lakes and on rivers such as the Missouri and the Mississippi. Usually the unfortunate passengers on the ice floe just ride it out. However, it can be more nerve-racking when your new 4x4 is sitting on the ice.

Ben East (1979) tells of the life threatening adventure of Lewis Street who was spearing trout through the ice of Lake Michigan as the ice broke loose. Street spent a cold week in January on the ice before he was able to walk and crawl to safety.

Precautions

Using common sense is the best advice to make a fishing trip on the ice a safe one. Check beforehand to learn where springs, inlets, aerators, and known thin ice are. Stay off unfamiliar areas. Know how to get out of a vehicle if it does go through and know how to rescue someone else who has fallen through the ice.

Small children and their mothers are often afraid of falling in the darkhouse hole. I suppose if you have a tendency to fall off chairs, you might fall in the hole! Or if the floor is icy, crowded with junk, or you just get excited you might go in the hole. In any case, it would be difficult to fall all the way in and not be able to get out.

Don't let this happen to you.

CHAPTER 15

Summary and Conclusions

You should now have a greater appreciation for spearing — its history, in practice, "how-to," and the controversial issues. I have learned a lot about spearing in the process of writing this book. The book idea came because I was concerned that spearing might soon be outlawed in Minnesota. Now, many years later, I am still concerned but have found other states to spear in, and much to my surprise, North Dakota has legalized darkhouse spearing.

Origin

The precise origin of darkhouse spearing was not pinned down in Chapter 2. However, it is clear that spearing in general was widespread. I like to think it began in North America, maybe even around the Great Lakes.

Across the Seven States

Rules governing darkhouse spearing vary across the seven states, just as do some of the practices. Minnesota stands alone in number of spearers and the controversy surrounding spearing. Other states provide more legal opportunities for spearing by allowing nonresidents to spear and allowing more species to be taken from a darkhouse.

The Controversy

Spearing will remain controversial as long as there are unlimited demands on limited resources. But, since spearing is a legitimate sport, there ought to be ways to modify the rules to accommodate as many sportsmen as possible, spearers included. If the problem is fish numbers, then the rational solutions lie in limits, license quotas, barbless hooks, and seasons. If the problem is fish sizes, then the solutions are trophy tags (for all anglers, not just for spearers), trophy lakes, or single-method lakes (e.g., spearing would be the only method allowed in some lakes).

Bob Strand, DNR regional fisheries supervisor at Bemidji, Minnesota, believes spearing will phase out within the next 5 to 10 years as the older generation dies. Younger people are more in tune with catch-and-release and fewer are taking up spearing (Rafftery 1988). If spearing dies a natural death, OK, but it would be a loss to future generations of spearers.

In Practice

Spearing is as much a tradition as are many other practices passed on among families in the spearing states. It is a great education and a way to learn about fish behavior. Time in the darkhouse is quality time to think. I have many fond memories of the days I have spent in the fishhouse.

The equipment spearers use is most often simple and utilitarian. Although equipment varies from a bare bones canvas shelter with a spear and decoy, to fancy darkhouses on wheels with all the amenities. Artificial decoys, "fish," are already highly prized collectors' items, spears might be next.

Eating Northerns

Most anglers scorn the northern and refuse to eat them. They're missing a real treat. In fact, there are few fish more tasty than a 5-pound snot rocket taken out of cold water.

Baked fish. Should you get the urge to spear a northern over about 7 pounds, try baking it. The first step is to scale it — do this outside so the scales don't end up all over the house. Then cut the head and tail off. You may want to filet the last 8 or 10 inches toward the tail and fry that another time. Cut the white belly off and take the guts out. You can then inspect the stomach to see what the fish ate last. I've found frogs, sunfish, perch, bass, crappies, northerns, tullibees, and all sorts of other unidentified fish parts. The larger fish will usually have two large egg sacks, most pronounced for the few months prior to April. Now, rinse well in cold water. Soak it in salt water overnight in the refrigerator, or freeze it in saltwater for later. Place the fish, right side up, on a baking pan and stuff as desired. Sprinkle your choice of spices over it and cover with bacon strips and lemon slices. Bake uncovered for about 60 minutes, or until it flakes easily from the backbone. Serve with fresh lemon juice or melted butter.

Fried fish. The best eating fish in Midwest lakes are northerns from 3 to 6 pounds. Filet them as you would any fish. Remove the rib bones with the filet knife. Remove the Y-bones if you like, but they aren't a problem with experienced fish eaters. Cut the filets into 3- to 4-inch wide pieces. Cover the pieces with a dry mixture of flour, salt, pepper, and other seasonings as desired; or use a store-bought fish batter. Drop the fish pieces into a ½ inch of hot, but not too hot, butter in a cast iron pan. If it isn't hot, the fish will stick to the pan. Fry for 10 minutes then turn the pieces over for another 5 minutes. Turn up the heat for the last few minutes for a crispy, golden brown coating. The bottom (from the fish's perspective) of each piece will be bone-free, since you took the rib bones out. The tail pieces of the filet will also be bone free. Break the top half of what you have left in two lengthwise. The top of that piece will also be bone free. The dreaded Y-bones will all be sticking up from the bottom half of that piece — pull them out and enjoy.

Epilogue

The world is getting to be a smaller place, with more people and seemingly fewer resources to go around — there are no more lakes in Minnesota or in Michigan or in Wisconsin than there were 100 years ago. The world's population has more than doubled since I was born and it is likely to double again before I die (if I'm lucky enough to live that long!). Yet, there are no more lakes. More people, with more leisure time and more money will inevitably bring changes to our consumptive recreation activities. Darkhouse spearing could fit within this constrained world along with hook-and-line fishing.

A writer who called ice fishing "the moronic sport" in 1978 (Chatham) also said it was in danger of being outlawed. I think he was wrong on both counts. In fact, the North Dakota Legislature passed a bill to allow darkhouse spearing in that state. North Dakota has a great abundance of prairie lakes that go through cycles of high water with lots of fast growing northern pike and perch followed by dryer periods of low water and winterkill. As of January 2001 there were about twice as many "lakes" that supported sportfishing as there were a decade earlier. The Legislature was wise to allow spearing as another means of harvesting northerns in these lakes, before water levels go back down and many of these lakes winterkill.

Jake introduced me to spearing many years ago. He died on the ice of Otter Tail Lake just days before Christmas in 1987. He lived his life to spear in the darkhouse. I hope this book helps to educate people about darkhouse spearing and contributes to keeping it legal.

SUMMARY AND CONCLUSIONS

References and Credits

References

Adler, Mortimer J. 1990. *Reforming Education: The Opening of the American Mind.* MacMillian Publishing Company, New York.

Alaska Department of Fish and Game. 1986. *1986 Alaska Sport Fishing Regulations Summary.* Juneau, Alaska.

Alt, Kenneth. 1984. "The Northern Pike in Alaska." Wildlife notebook series, Alaska Department of Fish and Game, Fairbanks.

"An Unrestricted Record." *Field and Stream* October 1990, page 60.

Arnson, Rossans. 1986. *The Effects of Tourism on the Local Economy: A survey of Business Establishments in the Cass Lake Area.* Minnesota Center for Survey Research, University of Minnesota, Minneapolis.

Baltezore, J. and Jay A. Leitch. 1987. *Attitudes of Minnesota Anglers.* Report to Minnesota Department of Natural Resources by Center for Environmental Studies, Tri-College University, Fargo, North Dakota.

Baron, Frank R. 1990. "Ice Decoy Sell List." No. 18 (Winter), Livonia, Michigan.

Baron, Frank R. 1989. "Ice Decoy Sell List." No. 11 (Winter), Livonia, Michigan.

Baron, Frank R. 1988. "Ice Decoy Sell List." No. 10 (Fall), Livonia, Michigan.

Baron, Frank R. 1986. "Ice Decoy Sell List." No. 1 (Summer) and No. 2 (Fall), Livonia, Michigan.

Baumann, Paul C. and James Jaeger. 1983. *Freshwater Fisherman's Companion.* Van Nostrand Reinhold Company, New York.

Bauer, Erwin A. 1958. "Shanty Caviar." *Outdoor Life* 121(2): 44-47, 92, 93.

Bergh, Kit. 1975. *Northern Pike Fishing: The Angler's Complete Handbook.* Dillon Press, Inc., Minneapolis.

Beskin, Gerald. 1951. "The Lucky Stick." *Sports Afield.*

Bethel, Lawrence. 1987. Decoy carver, Park Rapids, Minnesota (personal communication).

Beyerle, George B. 1971. "Management of an impoundment containing a population of slow growing norther pike." Job 6, Project No. F-29-R-4, final report, Department of Natural Resources, Lansing, Michigan.

Borge, Lila U. and Jay A. Leitch. 1988. *Winter Darkhouse Spearing in Minnesota: Characteristics of Participants.* Misc. Pub. #2, Center for Environmental Studies, Tri-College University, Fargo, North Dakota.

Boulanger, Tom. 1971. *An Indian Remembers: My Life as a Trapper in Northern Manitoba.* Peguis Publishers, Winnipeg.

Brazier, Jerry. 1985. *Ice Fishing Guide.* Ice Fishing Publications, Thief River Falls, Minnesota.

Breining, Greg. 1994. "Something Fishy." *The Minnesota Volunteer* Jan-Feb:20-27.

Busiahn, Thomas R. 1990. *Chippewa Treaty Harvest of Natural Resources — Wisconsin, 1983-1990.* Great Lakes Indian Fish & Wildlife Commission, Odanah, Wisconsin.

Busiahn, Thomas, Neil Kmiecik, Jim Thannum, and Jim Zorn. 1989. *1989 Chippewa Spearing Season — Separating Myth from Fact.* Great Lakes Indian

Fish & Wildlife Commission, Odanah, Wisconsin.

Causey, Ann S. 1989. "On the Morality of Hunting." *The International Journal of Applied Philosophy 11(Winter):327-343.*

Chalmers, A.F. 1982. *What is this thing called Science?* University of Queensland Press, New York.

Chatham, Russell. 1978. *Silent Seasons: 21 Fishing Adventures by 7 American Experts.* E.P. Dutton, New York.

Chiappetta, Jerry. 1966. *Modern ABC's of Ice Fishing.* Stackpole Books, Harrisburg, Pennsylvania.

Chihuly, Mike. 1983. "Spearing for Whitefish." *Alaska Outdoors* 6(5): 18-19, 21-23.

Densmore, Frances. 1979 (reprint edition). *Chippewa Customs.* Minnesota Historical Society Press, St. Paul, Minnesota. (Originally published in 1929 as Bulletin 86 by the Bureau of American Ethnology.)

Dornbrook, Don. 1948. "Hunting Big Fish Under the Ice." *Popular Mechanics* 89(2): 148-151, 236, 240, 246.

Doxey, Michael R. 1987. Sport Fish Division, Alaska Department of Fish and Game, photocopied flyer entitled "Ice fishing shanty information sheet." Fairbanks.

East, Ben. 1979. *Frozen Terror.* Crestwood House, Inc.

East, Ben. 1959. "Row over Pike Spearing." *Outdoor Life* 12391) 18-19.

Eddy, Samuel and James C. Underhill. 1969. *How to know the freshwater fishes.* Third Edition. Wm. C. Brown Company Publishers, Dubuque, Iowa.

Emmett, Jim. 1938. "Fishing Beneath the Frozen Waters." *St. Nicholas* 65(3):40-41.

Esarey, Duane. 1993. "The Ancient Art of Decoy Fishing." *The Living Museum* 55(1):5-8.

Needham, Robert G. 1986. Letter of March 5. Regional fisheries manager, Montana Department of Fish, Wildlife & Parks, Glasgow.

Ormstad, Olav and Knut Rom. 1972. *Isfiske (Ice Fishing),* Cappalen, Oslo, Norway.

Outdoor Outlines. 1987. "New DNR spearing study shows less pike taken than in 1981 endeavor. April 9, p. 12.

Peterson, Jim 1985. "Editorials." *Outdoor News,* February 22.

Phillips, Angus. 1986. "Spearing for Pike in the Heart of the 'Soo'." *The Washington Post* page D3, February 5.

Plein, J.F. 1936. "Eels of the Yukon." *The Alaska Sportsman* 2(3):10,21.

Radcliffe, William. 1921. *Fishing from the Earliest Times.* Burt Franklin, New York.

Rafftery, Gerry. 1988. "Spearing on the way out?" *The Forum* July 3, p. E10.

Rau, Ron. 1977. "The Day the Pike Put the Move on Herman." *Sports Illustrated* 46(1):38-41.

Reiger, George. 1988. "Over-Ruled!" *Field & Stream* 42(11):21, 24, 25.

Richey, Dave. 1990. "Ugly sturgeon mostly leave empty feeling." *The Detroit News* pp. 8A, 8D, February 6.

Rostlund, Erhard. 1952. *Freshwater Fish and Fishing in Native North America.* Publications in Geography, Volume 9, University of California Press, Berkeley.

Ruggiero, Vincent R. 1988. *Teaching Thinking Across the Curriculum.* Harper & Row, Publishers, New York.

Schroeder, Joseph J., Jr. (ed.). 1969. *1908 Sears, Roebuck Catalogue.* (replica) Follett Publishing Company, Chicago.

Sears, Roebuck & Co. 1908. *Catalogue No. 117.* Chicago.

Sonnenburg, Dave. Undated. "Case Study, Spearing Northern Pike: A Sport or Not?" Education Section, Bureau of Information and Education, Minnesota Department of Natural Resources, St. Paul.

South Dakota 1990 Fishing Handbook. 1990. Department of Game, Fish and Parks, Pierre.

Stark, Larry and Magnus Berglund. 1990. *Hook, Line and Shelter.* Adventure Publications, Inc.,Cambridge, Minnesota.

REFERENCES AND CREDITS

Swenson, Brad. 1986. "Cass Lake spearing ban opposed." *The (Bemidji) Pioneer* Aug. 3.

Talsma, Art. 1988. Director Wildlife Division, State of South Dakota, Department of Game, Fish and Parks, Pierre (personal communication).

Thannum, Jim. 1990. *1990 Chippewa Spearing Season — Conflict and Cooperation.* Great Lakes Indian Fish & Wildlife Commission, Odanah, Wisconsin.

Thomas, Jerry. 1989. *"When your car falls through the ice."* Minnesota Sportsman 1989(1):44-47.

Treat, Craig P. 1987. "The winter sport fishery of Buffalo, Howard, and Waverly Lakes, Wright County." F9-R(P)-5, Study 5, Minnesota Department of Natural Resources, St. Paul.

Trench, Charles Chenevix. 1974. *A History of Angling.* Follett Publishing Company, Chicago.

Von Brandt, Andres. 1964. *Fish Catching Methods of the World.* Fishing News (Books) Ltd., London.

Walcheck, Ken. 1974. "Ice Fishing: 'Hot' Pastime for a Cold Day." *Montana Outdoors* 5(1):19-26.

Warren, William W. 1984. *History of the Ojibway People.* Minnesota Historical Society Press, St. Paul, Minnesota. (First edition was published in 1885.)

Wheeler, Robert C. 1985. *A Toast to the Fur Trade: A Picture Essay on Its Material Culture.* Wheeler Productions, St. Paul, Minnesota.

Wilcox, Alvin H. 1907. *A Pioneer History of Becker County, Minnesota.* Pioneer Press Company, St. Paul, Minnesota.

William Mills & Son. 1905. *Catalogue — William Mills & Son — Fishing Tackle.* New York.

Wisconsin Department of Natural Resources. 1991. *Guide to Wisconsin Hook and Line Fishing Regulations 1991.* PUBL-FM-301, Madison.

Wisconsin Department of Natural Resources. 1991. *Wisconsin Spearing & Netting Regulations.* Madison.

Wisner, Bill. 1983. *The Fishermen's Source Book.* MacMillan Publishing Co., Inc., New York.

Wolverton, Chuck. 1989. (Memo dated February 6). Big Rapids, Michigan.

Zumbro, Jim. 1978. *Icefishing, East and West.* McKay Co., New York.

Technical References

Hotchkiss, Neil. 1972. *Common Marsh, Underwater & Floating-leaved Plants of the United States and Canada.* Dover Publications, Inc., New York.

Needham, James G. and Paul R. Needham. 1962. *A guide to the study of Fresh-Water Biology.* Holden-Day, Inc., San Francisco.

Peterka, John. 1991. Zoology professor, North Dakota State University, Fargo (personal communication).

Scott, W.B. and E.J. Crossman. 1973. *Freshwater Fishes of Canada.* Fisheries Research Board of Canada, Ottawa.

Walden, Howard T. 1964. *Familiar Freshwater Fishes of America.* Harper & Row, Publishers, New York.

Credits

Cover

"Darkhouse Action" by Les Kouba, print available from Wildlife Art Galleries, Minneapolis, Minnesota.

Photos

Oliver Aune, p. 9

Gary Harrington, p. 4

Duey Johnston, pp. 54, 69, 133, 134

Bill Lambert, p. 99

Minnesota DNR, p. 147

Troy Schroeder, p. 93

Ralph Woods, p. 92

Drawings

Frank Baron, p. 15, 52

Debbie Tanner, pp. 8, 10, 11, 12, 20, 36, 37, 45, 46, 48, 49, 56, 58, 59, 65, 74, 77, 142, 144

Cartoon

Minneapolis/St. Paul Star Tribune, p. 118

ORGANIZED 1986

Join the Minnesota Darkhouse & Angling Association, Organized in 1986. Annual membership is (in January 2001): $10, or $5 for youth membership (16 & under). Life memberships are $250, and include a limited edition Les C. Kouba print. Contact the Association office at P.O. Box 1875, Burnsville, MN 55337, or one of the local chapters for more information. The Association web site is www.mndarkhouse.org.

There are ten MD&AA chapters across the state.

Central Chapter of MD&AA
(St. Cloud area)
204 Buffalo St.
Delano, MN 55328

Metro Chapter of MD&AA
P.O. Box 1875
Burnsville, MN 55337

Brainerd Lakes Chapter of MD&AA
501 Lynndale Dr. North
Baxter, MN 56425

Itasca Chapter of MD&AA
(Grand Rapids area)
P.O. Box 1875
Burnsville, MN 55337

East Otter Tail Chapter of MD&AA
RR 2, Box 252
New York Mills, MN 56567

Paul Bunyan/Northern Chapter of MD&AA
(Cass Lake area)
51441 Wolf Ridge Rd.
Cass Lake, MN 56633

Lakes Chapter of MD&AA
608 Broadway Ave.
Detroit Lakes, MN 56501

Lake Superior Chapter of MD&AA
6106 Arnold Rd.
Duluth, MN 55803

Park Rapids Chapter of MD&AA
17964 119th Ave.
Park Rapids, MN 56470

Southern Lakes Chapter of MD&AA
230 7th Ave. SE
Waseca, MN 56093

Our Mission Statement:

To educate and teach the public of the heritage and methods of darkhouse spearfishing. The methods of using artificial decoys to take fish through the ice dates back hundreds of years to the Native Americans of our region and it's practice continues through today. (continued on next page)

We are dedicated to expose people of all ages to our sport and our historical ties with this ancient tradition, to promote their participation and continuance, and to encourage the bonding that this heritage creates between our citizens and our natural resources.

We are also comitted to protecting and preserving our sport and historical rights for all people and for all times, while promoting the responsible use of our renewable fish resources.